Self-harm, secrets and lies

A personal workbook

Elaine Fogarty

chimpmunkapublishing
the mental health publisher

Elaine Fogarty

All rights reserved, no part of this publication may be reproduced by any means, electronic, mechanical photocopying, documentary, film or in any other format without prior written permission of the publisher.

> Published by
> Chipmunkapublishing
> United Kingdom

http://www.chipmunkapublishing.com

Copyright © Elaine Fogarty 2016

ISBN 978-1-78382-296-6

About Chipmunkapublishing

Mental health books give a voice to writers with mental illness around the world. At Chipmunkapublishing we raise awareness of mental health and the stigma surrounding mental health problems by encouraging society to listen. We are documenting mental health literature as a genre so history does not forget the survivors and carers of people with mental illness and disabilities.

Self-harm, secrets and lies

For

**She who never once gave up on me
&
He who helped me find my wings**

Elaine Fogarty

Author Biography

At the young age of just 13, Elaine was struggling with dark thoughts, and wrote the poem 'suicide'; her poetry and scribbled journal notes were a valued means of expression and exploration. In coming years she started to self-harm regularly and in her 20's began to receive periodic treatment for depression. Elaine found herself in suicidal crisis three times over following years but survived each by the grace of a stranger. In 2006 she found herself back in that darkest of places and so decided to make a stand; she gathered journal notes and sat nervously with her GP. After four weeks on a psychiatric ward, the demon was finally named - bipolar II. The self-harm continued as Elaine tried to come to terms with her new diagnosis.

Elaine acknowledges her bipolar disorder, anxiety issues, self-harm and OCD. She denies them strength born of secrecy choosing instead to be totally open about her mental illness and use this voice to help others. To date Elaine has been in suicidal crisis seven times and has lived almost 40 years with her dependency on self-harm.

Elaine was born in 1967 in Portadown, Northern Ireland. She has been with her Husband Colin over 30 years and still lives in her hometown with him and her two cats Flash & Figaro: she enjoys film and theatre, computer projects, good food shared with good friends, and the sense of connection afforded her by social networking online. Elaine currently works in domiciliary care and as one of her most effective self-care tools is participation in learning, she continues to explore the world of correspondence courses and college night classes.

Since writing her last book "Diary of a bipolar survivor" Elaine not only continues her efforts as advocate for mental health discussion but has since trained and set up a small Relaxation & CBT therapy practice that specialises in stress and anxiety management. She designs and delivers courses and workshops around mindfulness and other wellness tools and is honoured to maintain a blog on the subject of mental health. Elaine recognises the substantial contribution made

Self-harm, secrets and lies

to her own personal growth and recovery by membership of The Mental Health Forum, finding it rewarding to act as part of the independent Service user voice that contributes to recovery focused planning and provision within her Health trust and beyond.

All of these activities have helped to subtly re-wire old associations and beliefs that held her back and by extension kept her dependant on self-harm as a primary coping tool; they offered perspective, encouraged and empowered. Elaine's engagement with each of these as they fell into place around her over the past couple of years has proven that choice is ever-present and life exists beyond stigma. Self-harm is still part of her life but it no longer drives her to secrecy and lies. Openness about her mental illness and self-harm experiences is now a means to healing in itself.

Elaine Fogarty

Preface

I could write a rambling narrative full of personal example and yet fall short of properly answering the many questions about self-harm; there are so many perspectives. They say the truth has 3 faces – your story, my story and the bare facts – the truth of self-harm is just as complex. What I have offered here is a way to help you explore your own story, to find your own truth. Along the way you will read excerpts from my own experience designed to remind you that you are not alone as you walk this journey and that self-harm is just something you currently do – it doesn't have to be who you are. I am not a mental health professional; what you will find here is informed by personal opinion and experience and the prompts in the workbook sections are designed from the perspective of someone who understands.

My relationship with self-harm changed only a few years ago when I began to accept personal responsibility, step up and get actively involved in my own care, and finally understand that recovery did not mean cure. Up until that point I had turned to harming myself as a means of exercising control over a world that seemed to enjoy pushing me to breaking point. It knew my weaknesses and it was unrelenting. I knew it wasn't what other people did. I knew it wasn't the socially accepted norm. I knew no one would really understand how perfectly self-harm worked and how badly I needed it, so I kept my secret for over half my life. When things began to overwhelm me the cuts, burns, scratches etc. rose up to protect me, acting as a pressure valve to purge the nameless and the frightening. You may find it difficult to believe but my self-harm behaviours actually helped keep me alive.

People with my particular mental illness are often predisposed to addictive personality traits and I also have an OCD diagnosis but these were just fuel for a fire lit way back in my early teens. I didn't call it self-harm all those years ago, that label only appeared when I began to realise I had a mental illness and started picking up the language of the various professionals I encountered. I didn't see it as self-destructive back then either, that label also arrived in

Self-harm, secrets and lies

therapeutic discussion. I felt guilt and shame during my transition into recovery but not for the self-harm behaviours themselves, no, rather for the deliberate choice I made to try and leave them behind. It left me terribly conflicted as if abandoning a dear friend in favour of a new acquaintance. Even though some do manage it in time, deep down I doubted I could ever totally let go. Still… I made the important decision to change.

You join me at an interesting and exciting time in my journey; these past two to three years have seen the influence of self-harm all but disappear from my life (Two, perhaps three very low-impact occurrences in a year as opposed to upwards of four in a week – some of which were quite substantial.) It is hoped that the honesty of this book will promote understanding for those who do not self-harm around how challenging this transition can be, but it remains primarily a tool for those who live daily with this challenge and the secrets and lies that come with it.

This book will not 'fix' you – you are not broken - but if you are ready to take on the challenge of personal responsibility and growth then it will support you.
Respond with total honesty as you work and you will get the most out of it.

Elaine Fogarty

This workbook belongs to

Date Started

Elaine Fogarty

Self-harm, secrets and lies

*** Personal responsibility ***

Management of your self-harm and other related issues is deeply dependant on your acceptance of personal responsibility; the things you make effort to learn and the decisions you make will all contribute to your very personal journey; this is how it should be. No one else can do this for you.

It begins with how you choose to use this book. What you see here is based on my own lived experience and the influence of others that have walked my journey with me. This will guide, inform, and challenge you but it should not be accepted without question – consider what you read carefully and be open to reflection and personal enquiry… actively seek out more information and build your own perspective.

This personal responsibility extends to the area of mental health treatment, medication and first aid in particular – I am not a trained medical or mental health professional and what you read here is based on my own lived experience and my own observations and learning. Everything is offered in good faith but you will need to clarify and verify such information before acting upon it – medical science, diagnosis, treatments, medications and first aid advice all change over time and you should always make sure you personally seek out the most up to date and accurate information. Personal responsibility is the essence of self-care.

You are an expert by your own lived experience but there is always more to learn and more ways to grow. It is my hope that this workbook will help you as you continue to reclaim responsibility and move with confidence into better management of both your self-harm and any underlying condition.

Elaine Fogarty

This workbook is designed to be as inconspicuous as possible; you may not be in a place right now that allows you to openly share your challenges or your efforts to understand and address them. This is OK.
This process is yours – the decisions around it are yours. Personal responsibility also means keeping yourself as safe as possible as you progress so to help you there is a list of support services at the back of this book that can be contacted anonymously at any time.

Self-harm, secrets and lies

** Possible Trigger **

The information and questions shared in this book are specifically about self-harm behaviour and should help explore the many ways in which it affects your life.

If you feel vulnerable you may wish to have a trusted friend or supporter sit with you at times. You may also find it useful to work with your key-worker or counsellor on this if you have one.

Please be aware

The author shares some unedited content from her own journals over the years and some of this is unapologetically raw and graphic. There are no photographs but you will encounter sketches and text which could possibly act as triggers.

As you complete the workbook sections you will also be recording your own deepest feelings and revealing some of your own most powerful triggers. Work always with patience and self-compassion. There is no time limit on personal growth

Elaine Fogarty

Sharing and therapeutic application

This workbook is protected by copyright.
If you wish to discuss authorised use of any section
you may contact the author directly via methods
listed in the final pages.

Table of contents

1 What is Self-harm?

2 My own Story

3 Author's perspective

4 Safe practice

5 Help available

6 My own notes

Elaine Fogarty

Elaine Fogarty

Self-harm, secrets and lies

Self-harm has many forms and is most often a coping mechanism itself, either releasing the overwhelming pain and pressure felt or exerting some measure of control in circumstances that feel totally beyond our ability to handle. Some differentiate and talk about self-injury and self-mutilation as well but for purpose of this book we will simply stay with the term "self-harm" as a generic. This practice is often deeply misunderstood and it can easily over-shadow its own root cause and leave a person isolated and conflicted. Sometimes those of us who practice self-harm will find each other and share stories. There is a certain acceptance and freedom in that and we can learn some good coping tools if the relationships stay healthy and supportive. Those of us who have shared our secret with friends or professionals may indeed have been given ideas on how to distract ourselves from harming behaviours or begin to replace them with other tools. Self-harming can however quickly become an addictive behaviour and this invites great secrecy and sometimes shame or guilt. The cycle can be very painful and destructive. Secrets, lies, judgement and isolation are a lot to deal with on top of all the underlying pain that cries out for relief. Make no mistake – trying to manage powerful self-harm urges is a lengthy struggle with many setbacks – but it *is* worth it.

Self-harm summons up images of cutting in the minds of most who hear the words but the range of different behaviours is quite large. The various types include but are not limited to deliberate burning or scalding, scratching and skin-picking, hair pulling, severe scratching or skin abrasions, friction burns, bone-breaking, deliberate hits or bangs, piercing of the skin, ingestion of harmful substances or objects, self-choking, cigarette burns, biting, extreme eating behaviours, self-starving, stopping wounds from healing, reckless behaviours, binging, instigating fights, taking drugs or abusing alcohol or other substances.

Elaine Fogarty

The reasons that drive a person to practice self-harm are equally varied and these include but are not limited to the need for simple comfort, the release of pressure and overwhelm, the need to address a sense of numbness, to address self-hatred, to replace internal pain with external pain, to become numb in the face of overwhelm or over-stimulation, to identify with and be accepted by peers, to simply act out, to manipulate others, to find clarity of thought, to prove to one's self that it is possible to survive, to seize control or as a means of attention-seeking or even as a cry for help. When time passes and the lines begin to blur self-harm can simply become an act driven by addiction. Somewhere along the line the brain just makes the connection between self-harm and the desired effect. The brain is a very powerful entity and such influence is difficult to negate.

The boundaries between suicidal ideation/attempts and severe and prolonged self-harm can also become blurred but it is a myth that self-harm is *always* a precursor to suicide and it is a myth that it is just the reserve of a misunderstood sub-culture or angst-ridden teenagers. It is also a myth that all those who self-harm are dangerous. The most common myth of all is that those who self-harm do so merely for attention and this is far removed from the truth – most people who self-harm live with it under a veil of secrecy and ever increasing and elaborate lies. Self-harm, secrets and lies conspire, compound and consume – they actually prefer to be invisible.

There are some very real risks to living with self-harm and apart from the obvious one of death itself, there are things to consider such as infections, risk of accidental serious injury, permanent scarring, nerve or tendon damage, limited movement due to severe scaring around joints, paralysis, psychological trauma, damaged or failed relationships, social losses, development of eating disorders, risk of

Self-harm, secrets and lies

becoming addicted to other behaviours or substances, medical trauma due to overdosing and of course the risk of exacerbating an existing mental health condition while actually attempting to ease distress. Self-harm may be self-destructive, ill-advised and mal-adaptive on many levels but despite all the risks people continue to use it as their main coping tool because quite simply – it works when nothing else they know will. Dealing with self-harm then is all about exploration of options and finding new and safer ways to achieve the same results.

To begin to deal with self-harm one must begin with basic coping techniques or tools and build an understanding of what works or does not work personally. The idea behind coping techniques is mainly to distract or to buy time and if possible substitute a behaviour that can go some way towards achieving a similar result to the self-harm itself. We who practice self-harm know from experience that such tools do not always work, or indeed continue to work in the long term, but through trial and error we have each found small ways to help ourselves in our personal circumstances. Some of the most effective coping tools I have used over the years would have been quite unusual even silly to an outsider, yet they worked at the time. Many of the techniques I still use on a regular basis are listed in the pages that follow and they each have value. Do they replace all my self-harm urges? No – but they help me manage them. I am not ashamed to admit that very occasionally I still think of self-harm when I become overwhelmed, but I do so now in a more controlled and safe manner and with far less frequency than in years past.

Over the years I have gathered quite a list of coping tools and techniques and they can be categorised into six main types – distract, buy time, pain substitute, visual cue, safe places and emotional purge. I have listed these below.

Elaine Fogarty

I owe a lot to the people who shared their techniques with me in the past. As I have progressed in my recovery journey and learned more about management of the illness itself I have also come to understand why I had a need to use self-harm. I admit that it was… is, an addictive behaviour that will always challenge me. I've used more and more of these tools as time goes on and I accept that I may always need them but I have chosen to step away from the secrets and lies. I no longer choose to hide the scars. If someone points and asks a question, I answer and if I have opportunity to educate or support, I do so. It's called 'paying it forward.'

Self-harm, secrets and lies

Mark here	Distraction
	Breath awareness
	Give yourself a facial or reshape and trim a beard
	Invite a friend round
	Cloud watching
	Plan a holiday or event
	Rearrange furniture
	Read a book
	Go for a bike ride
	Clean windows

	Go for a drive
	Use a mala and pray or chant
	Form drawing
	Bake or cook a meal
	Adult colouring books
	Do something nice for someone else
	Work on a jigsaw
	Blast the music loud and dance
	Tai-Chi
	Origami

Self-harm, secrets and lies

	Work on learning a new language
	Play solitaire
	Count – anything, wall tiles, grains of rice, words on a page
	Ring or message a friend
	Have a wardrobe or toolbox clear-out
	Play a musical instrument
	Wash the car
	Research something online
	Have a shower
	Watch an open fire burn

	Visit an online forum and answer queries
	Blow and pop bubble gum
	Play games on the phone/tablet
	Watch a candle burn
	Build with children's themed building blocks
	Watch a movie
	Doodle
	Do some housework
	Do some macro photography
	Mindfulness practice

Self-harm, secrets and lies

	Watch comedy video or instruction video online
	Go shopping
	Calligraphy
	Yoga
	Massage cream into hands and arms
	Apply a self-tan
	Play with a pet
Mark here	**Buy time**
	Place a temporary tattoo or draw (most commonly a butterfly) on the area you are considering harming then refrain from that harm until the tattoo has worn away.

	Break a glow stick and do not self-harm until it stops glowing completely
	Put a fake tattoo on the skin then slowly pick off again
	Set a timer on your mobile phone or use an egg timer
	Work on learning how to juggle, knit, crochet – any new skill
	Tear a paper page into lots of tiny little bits
	Polish some silver, brass or wood – maybe even the car
	Trim manicure and paint nails
	Meditate or use a guided recording to help focus the mind

Self-harm, secrets and lies

	Take a bubble bath
	Memorise a poem or some song lyrics
	Colour-coordinate your wardrobe
	Count back from 200
	Trial a new makeup look
	Build a card house
	Alphabetise the Book, CD or DVD collection
	Write a detailed step by step instruction list for how to tie a tie or do up shoe laces or make a cup of tea for example, so that anyone strictly following them would get the correct result
	Do a crossword or other puzzle

	Organise your photos/music on your phone or computer
Mark here	**Pain substitute**
	Put an elastic band around wrist and snap repeatedly
	Chew on some fresh ginger
	Rub or hold an ice cube to the skin
	Bite into a fresh chilli
	Eat a lemon
Mark here	**Visual cue**
	Create fake wounds with makeup or theatrical supplies

Self-harm, secrets and lies

	Place a dressing on skin even though there are no wounds
	Take a non-permanent red marker and go to town marking slashes on the skin
	Visualise the entire ritual in detail and focus on sensations
	Go through the whole ritual but stop short of actual harm
	Visualise wearing summer clothes with scarred skin
	Make some fake blood with food colouring and apply
	Draw cuts/wounds on a photograph of yourself
	Take your blade or tool to photographs

Elaine Fogarty

Mark here	Safe places
	Go somewhere very public if you are scared to be alone Go somewhere very quiet if you are over-stimulated
	Go to a place of worship
	Go to a shopping centre
	Go to a library
	Go to a multi-denominational quiet room in a hospital or similar
	Go to an art gallery or a museum
	Go to a support drop-in centre
	Go to the cinema

Self-harm, secrets and lies

	Go to a friend's house
	Go to the gym
	Go to a support group meeting
	Go to a coffee shop and read a book
Mark here	**Emotional purge**
	Punch a pillow or have a pillow fight with the wall
	Write, sketch, scrawl, express, vent
	Exercise vigorously
	Ring a helpline
	Talk, even shout back to the "voices"

Elaine Fogarty

	Write a letter and then shred or burn it
	Ring a friend
	Put on sturdy shoes and stomp cans flat
	Play a musical instrument
	Jump on a trampoline
	Blow up balloons and then pop them
	Stomp around in muddy puddles
	Use a carefully selected computer chat room
	Get a magazine and draw over the faces in the pictures
	Shout and scream

Self-harm, secrets and lies

	Smash some old crockery
	Write all the thoughts down then tear up the paper
	Cry unashamedly
	Sing loudly and perhaps even dance
	Smash a watermelon to pieces
	Use a stress ball
	Use a non-permanent pen and write words over your skin
	Write in a journal Or write creatively
	Hit a tree or a wall with a big strong stick

	Vigorously knead bread dough
	Pray
	Write a poem
	Slash some old clothing into rags
	Shout and swear and rant and vent at the mirror
	Drive nails into an old bit of wood
	Go for a run
	If experienced in meditation – use that
	Scream, shout, vocalise
	If need be – ring a helpline AGAIN – it's ok

Self-harm, secrets and lies

Mark here	Some of my own are

Elaine Fogarty

Self-harm, secrets and lies

Elaine Fogarty

Self-harm, secrets and lies

Elaine Fogarty

Self-harm, secrets and lies

Self-harm is understood to be self-destructive as well as inviting the secrets and lies that wear down relationships; it can be highly addictive and it can help perpetuate issues of poor self-esteem or limited confidence. Self-harm can cause a person to isolate themselves and avoid any efforts to discuss its influence. With all this known and widely accepted even by we who practice self-harm, you could be forgiven for wondering why so many continue to turn to it as a means of coping with life. The simple answer is of course that although a learned behaviour, we return to it over and over again because it is so effective. We may not be able to articulate the extent of that effective intervention to others but we know it to be real and relevant and essential in our lives. As time goes on we who self-harm get our identity all tied up in the practice and see our future overshadowed with the choice between it and unbearable distress – in short the self-harm presents itself unchallenged as "normal."

Reflecting on the issues around self-harm and our feelings about it is a valuable exercise. It may not bring obvious immediate benefit but the honest consideration of some simple questions can begin to help us understand ourselves a little better and understand the behaviour well enough to begin to challenge it and look for other more positive ways to achieve results. The process is slow but learning of all kinds, personal growth of all kinds, take effort and we owe ourselves that level of self-care. Real and positive change is entirely possible. Self-harm can be overcome.

The questions on the following pages will yield best results if done only one a day, perhaps even one a week, so that we get real and personal insight. Answer each question by writing in this book or journaling, use bullet points thought maps, poetry or art... then explore the issue as fully as possible. Work on your own or with someone else but be sure to write with complete honesty. By the time you finish the questions section you will have a wealth of material to read and re-read and to reflect further on. Gaining insight into your self-harm behaviours will prove really helpful in the long term as you dip your toe in the waters of positive change.

This is your story - there are no wrong answers.

The usual reflective cycle is –

Answer the question with basic descriptions

Write about your feelings in regard to this

Try to evaluate and weigh perspectives

Draw some kind of interim conclusion

Establish what if any learning there has been in this enquiry

Write about your planned action based on all this

In time, revisit the topic and reflect on changes or fresh insight

Self-harm, secrets and lies

How to use this book

"Some of the most powerful secrets and lies are the ones we tell ourselves"   Elaine Fogarty.

The following workbook has been written by someone with personal lived experience of self-harm, someone who has been there and who understands the things that are so very difficult to explain, the things we hold secret and the lies we tell. It is designed to guide you in breaking down some of these barriers and help you to learn the process of self-reflection. This process will encourage you to value and trust your own insight and allow you to better manage your self-harm issues. Work systematically through the pages that follow – do not be tempted to skip difficult sections or skip ahead to areas that look more interesting. The order in which you work will be as important as the work you actually do however timescale is up to you. You can do one question page a day or one per week or one per appointment with your counsellor or keyworker – find what is comfortable and productive and then move forward with commitment.

You will get out of this what you put in.

You can write and draw in the book itself or use a separate journal or pad to expand your answers and explore even more deeply any issues that may arise. Working in a separate place also has the added advantage of leaving many areas of the book clear for use at a future date allowing comparison and demonstration of progress and growth – again the choice is yours.

This is YOUR story

This is YOUR journey

Elaine Fogarty

Why I want to use this book

Date ....

Self-harm, secrets and lies

Reasons why NOW is the right time

Date ……………………………………..

🗒 One

🗒 Two

🗒 Three

🗒 Four

🗒 Five

Elaine Fogarty

My thoughts on self-harm

Date ....

Self-harm, secrets and lies

Elaine Fogarty

My thoughts on how others react to my self-harm

Date ……………………………………………

✎ It's difficult for me because …

Self-harm, secrets and lies

✎ But sometimes …

Elaine Fogarty

What I can remember about my first time

Date ....

Self-harm, secrets and lies

This is a drawing to sum up how I felt that first time …

Date ....

Elaine Fogarty

I turned to self-harm that first time because...

Date ....

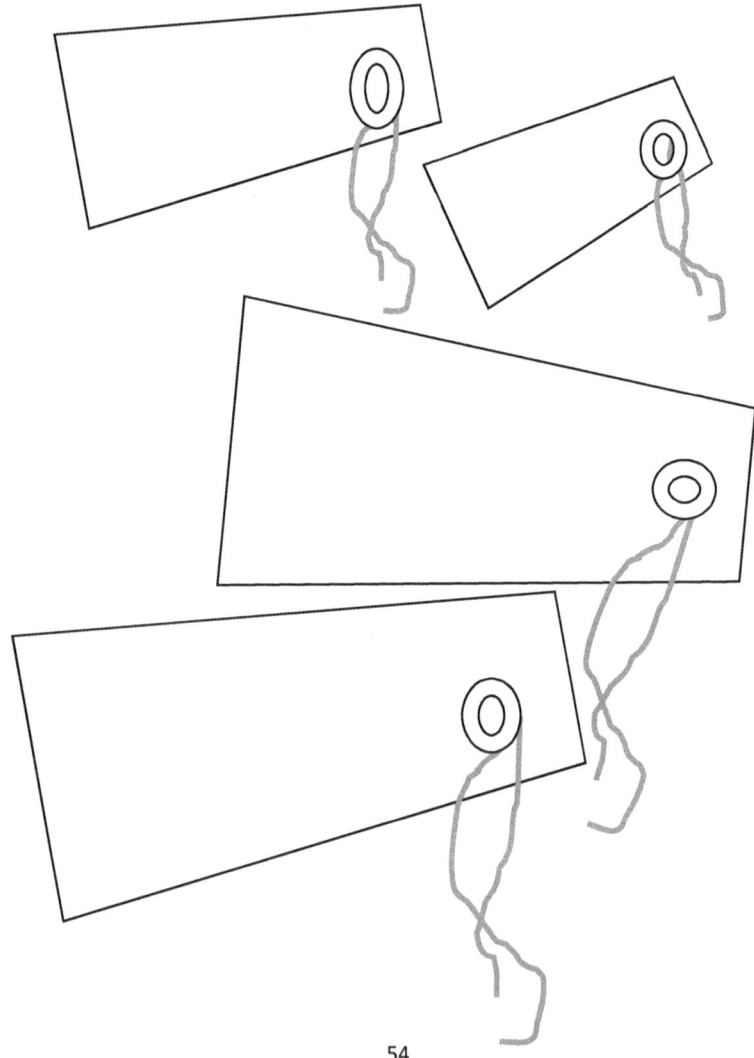

My thoughts during that first incident of self-harm…

Date ....

✎ I can remember thinking about …

My emotions that first time I harmed…

Date ……………………………………

📝 Before

📝 During

📝 After

Self-harm, secrets and lies

What I noticed immediately after that first time...

Date ....

....
....
....
....
....
....
....

....
....
....
....
....
....
....
....

Reflection on why I started to self-harm

Date ....

Self-harm, secrets and lies

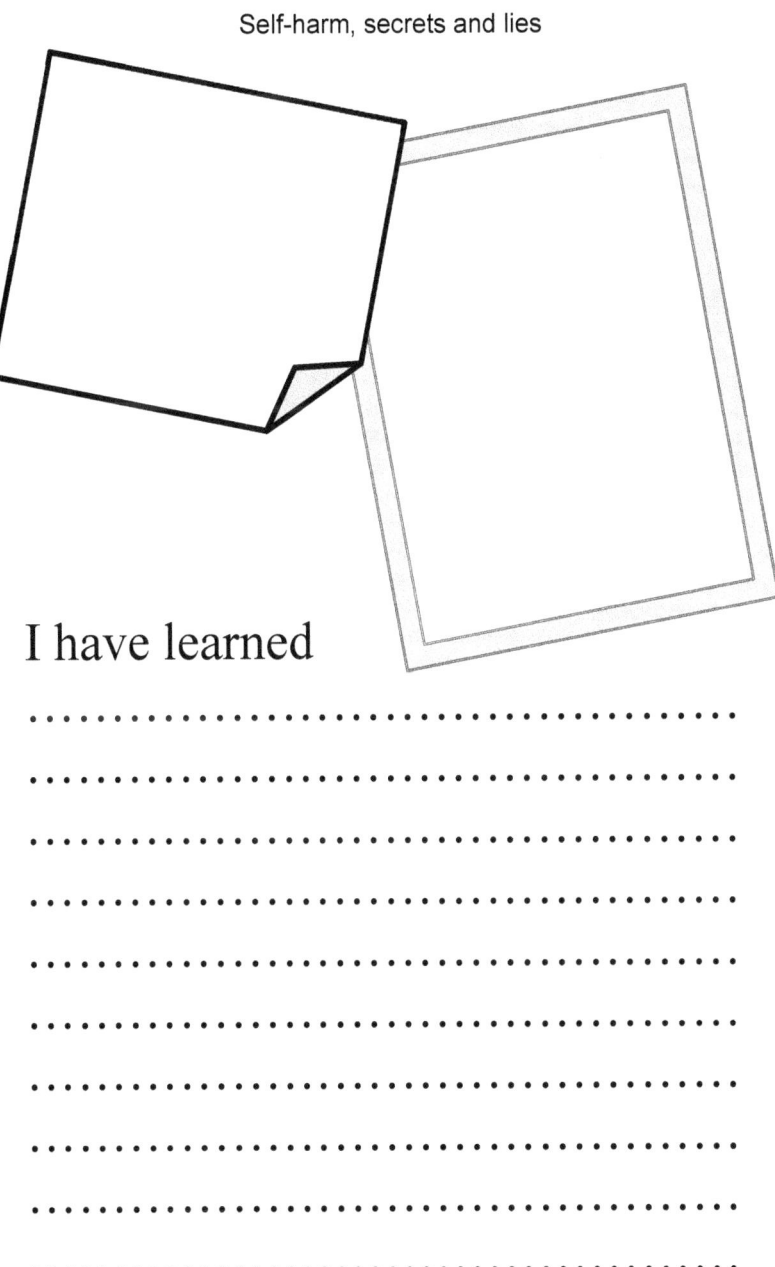

I have learned

....
....
....
....
....
....
....
....
....
....

What is difficult about thinking this way?

....

What is easy about thinking this way?

....

Self-harm, secrets and lies

Continued reflection…

Elaine Fogarty

The last time I turned to self-harm…

Date ....

✎ What I did

✎ What happened just before hand?

✎ Where I physically was just before hand

Self-harm, secrets and lies

✍ What I was feeling just beforehand

✍ What I was thinking just beforehand

Breaking it down

Thinking about that last time

✍ How I felt immediately afterwards

✍ My thoughts immediately afterwards

Elaine Fogarty

Date ....

What's real for me?

This has helped me identify the following trigger(s)	This has helped me identify the following difficult situation(s)

This is a drawing to sum up how I felt that last time …

Date ……………

The last time I turned to self-harm...

Date ....

Once I started, my self-harm happened exactly as I planned   Yes / No

....
....
....
....
....

Once I started, the self-harm actually achieved its goal   Yes / No

....
....
....
....
....

Self-harm, secrets and lies

Looking back – what could I have done differently…

Date ……………………

Elaine Fogarty

Reflection on why I turned to self-harm last time

Self-harm, secrets and lies

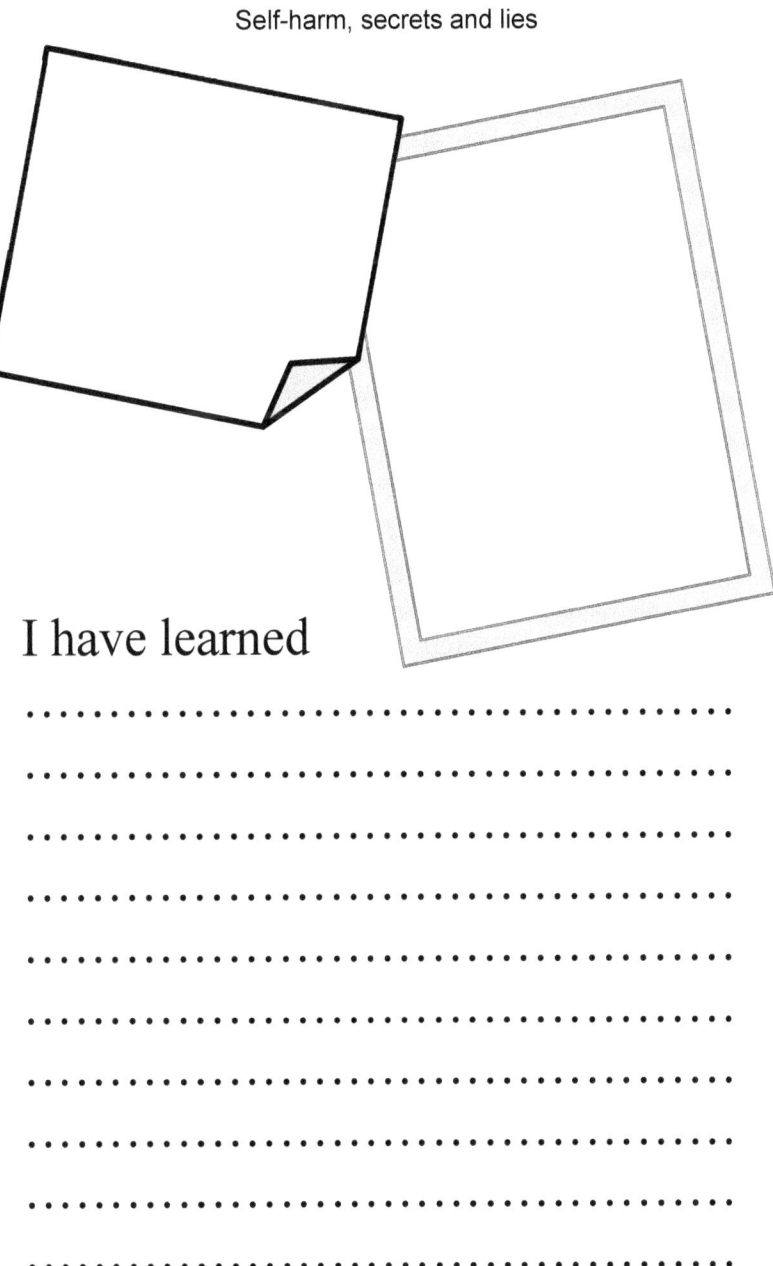

I have learned

....
....
....
....
....
....
....
....
....
....

What is difficult about thinking this way?

What is easy about thinking this way?

Self-harm, secrets and lies

Continued reflection…

Elaine Fogarty

Emotions connected to my self-harm are circled here…

Date …………………..

Pleasure

Fear   Nothing at all

Relief   Curiosity

Release   Arousal

Calmnes

Anger   Bliss

Remorse

Satisfaction

Confusion

Conflicted   Excitement

Craving attention

Pride

Feeling alive

Courage

Surprise   Relaxation

Welcoming pain   Disgust

Frustration

Stubbornnes

Anxiety   Self-Hatred

… Or … Write in your own

Self-harm, secrets and lies

The different ways I have deliberately harmed myself…

Date ………………………………..

Elaine Fogarty

How I judged which ways worked and which did not…

Date ……………………………………..

✍ How my brain made sense of it all as I started to habitually self-harm and my needs, tools and rituals developed.

Self-harm, secrets and lies

What was different about the ways that did not work...

Date ....

✍ How my brain made sense of it all as I started to habitually self-harm and my needs, tools and rituals developed.

Elaine Fogarty

How my attitude to self-harm has changed over time…

Date ………………………………..

✍ How my brain made sense of it all as I started to habitually self-harm and my needs, tools and rituals developed.

Self-harm, secrets and lies

The labels I give myself because of my self-harm are…

Date ……………………………………..

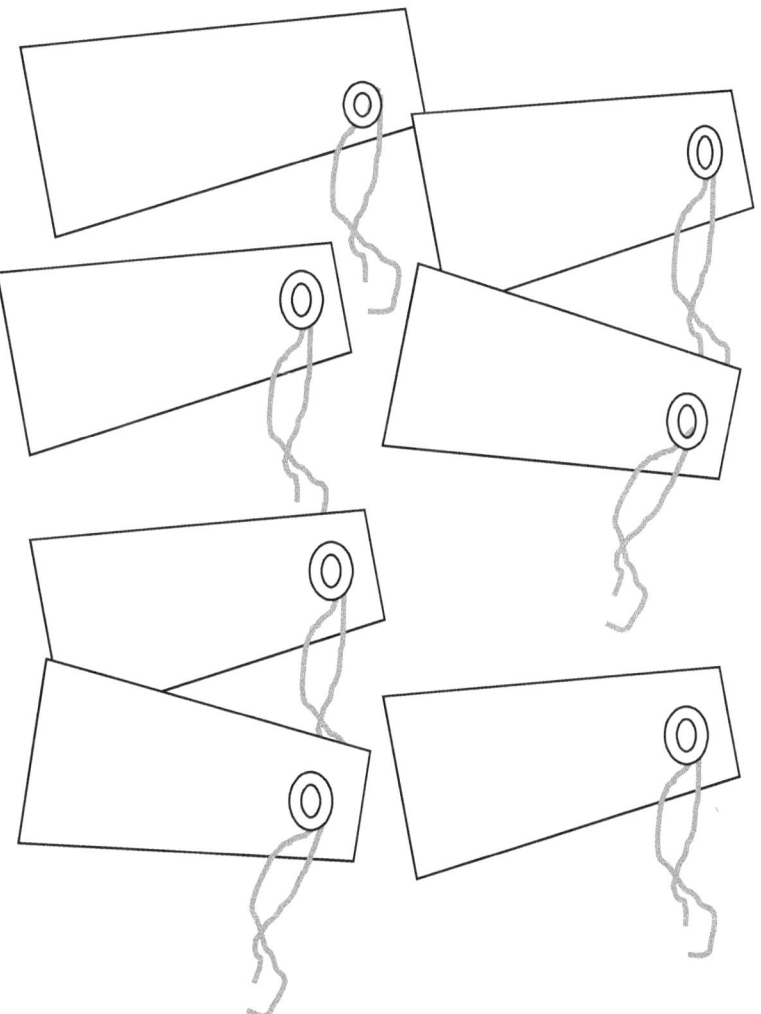

The labels others give me because of my self-harm are…

Date ……………………………………….

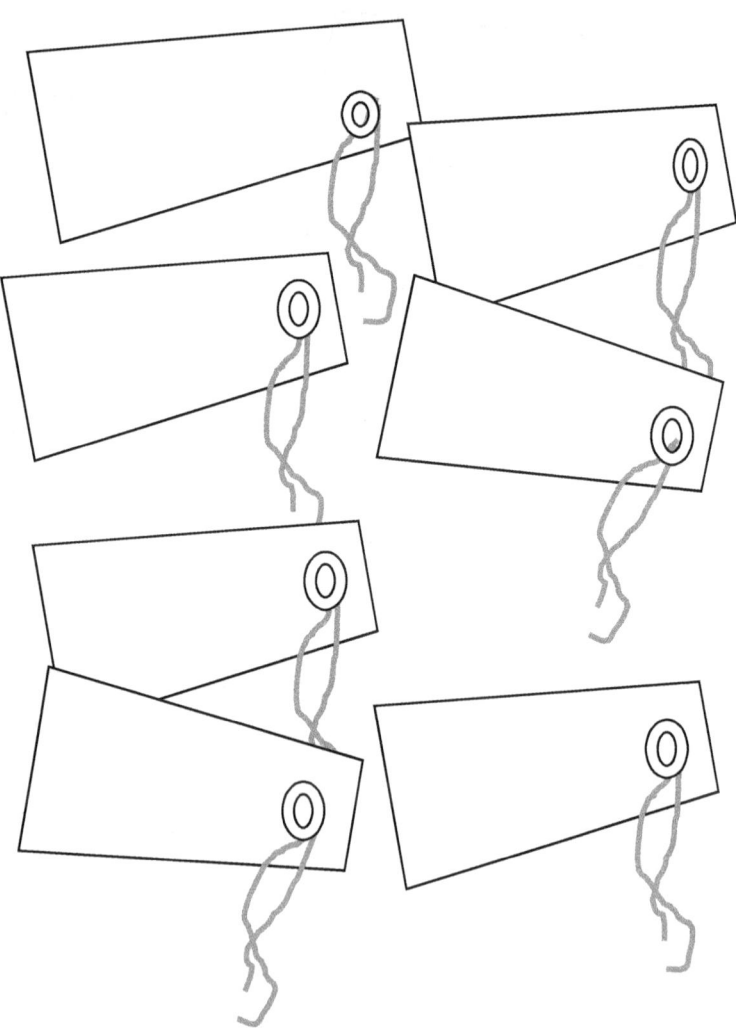

Self-harm, secrets and lies

I would describe my self-harm ritual like this…

Date ……………...……………………………..

This is a drawing to sum up the detail of my self-harm ritual …

Date ………………………

Self-harm, secrets and lies

What my scars mean to me...

Date ……………………………………

Elaine Fogarty

Thinking more deeply about my scars…

Date ……………………………………….

- How I feel about my scars being visible to others

- How I feel about the type/ appearance of my scars

- Why I choose the areas I do when I self-harm

- Practical problems my scars can cause

Self-harm, secrets and lies

What I wish people would understand about my scars…

Date …………………………………….

Elaine Fogarty

How I deal with questions about my scars…

Date ……………………………………..

Self-harm, secrets and lies

Date ....

If I was watching a friend struggle and consider self-harm… this is what I would say, what I would do

Date ....

> If I was watching a friend struggle and consider self-harm… this is what I would think, what I would feel

Self-harm, secrets and lies

What is different about how I treat myself...

Date ....

✍ These are the differences as I see them... not anyone else.

Elaine Fogarty

These are my thoughts on the secrets I've kept...

Date ……………………………………..

Self-harm, secrets and lies

These are my thoughts on the lies I have told…

Date ……………………………………….

What if I could time travel…

Date ……………………………………..

If I could go back and speak to my younger self on that day when I first thought to use self-harm as a tool, I would say

……………………………………………………………

……………………………………………………………

……………………………………………………………

……………………………………………………………

……………………………………………………………

If I could go back and speak to my younger self on that day when I first thought to use self-harm as a tool, I would also…

……………………………………………………………

……………………………………………………………

……………………………………………………………

……………………………………………………………

……………………………………………………………

……………………………………………………………

**If I sit quietly a while and think about a person I really like and respect, picture them sitting with me in that space as I prepare to self-harm... I wonder...
If they could not intervene but could only speak, what would they have to say to me?**

Date ……………………………..…………….

Reflection on the deeper questions of self-harm

Date ....

Self-harm, secrets and lies

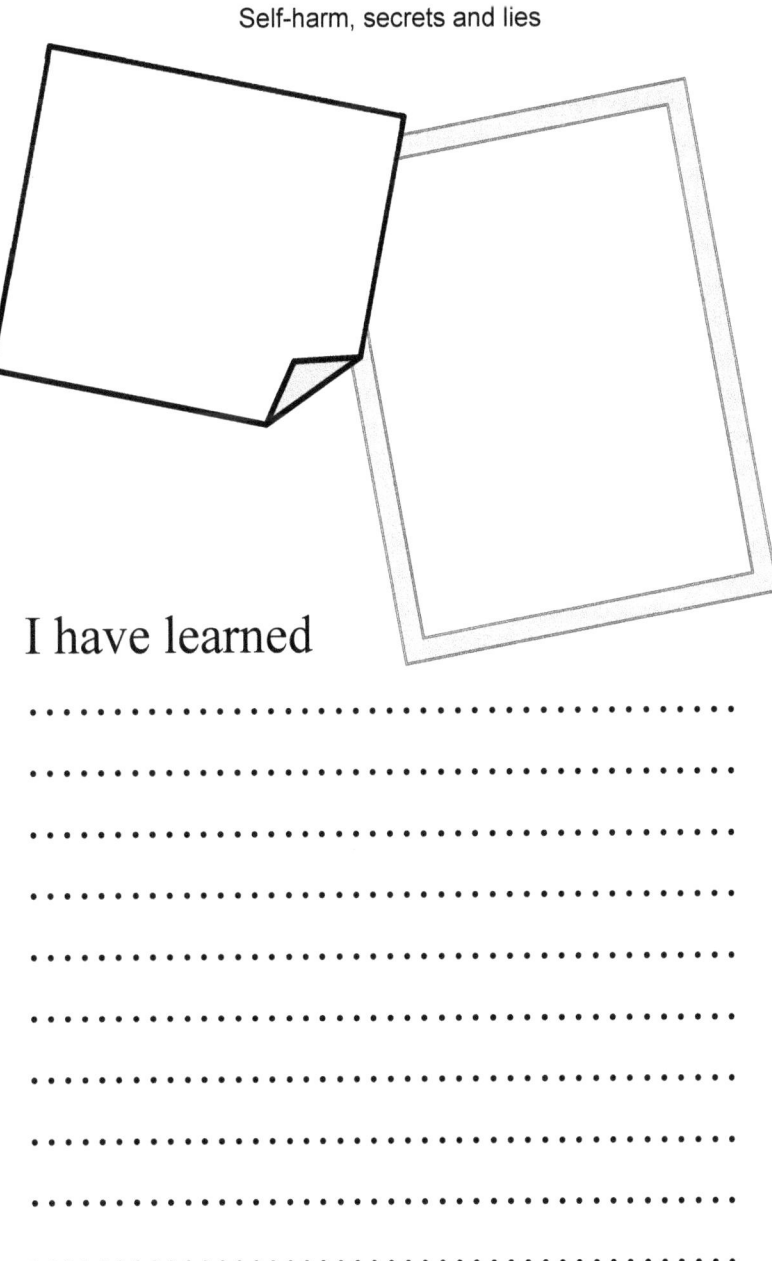

I have learned

....
....
....
....
....
....
....
....
....
....

What is difficult about thinking this way?

What is easy about thinking this way?

… **Continued reflection…**

ముందుగా ఎక్కడ

What people just don't understand about me is...

Date ....

If everyone would just stop telling me what to do with my life I could get on with the stuff that is important to me…

Date ……………………………………….

Elaine Fogarty

If I had the chance to try, I know I would be really good at ..

Date ....

....
....
....
....
....
....
....
....
....
....
....
....
....
....
....

If I could deal with life without needing to harm myself then…

Date ………………………………..

Elaine Fogarty

When my thoughts play tricks on me I start to believe...

Date ....

....
....
....
....
....
....
....
....
....
....
....
....
....
....
....

When my emotions get overwhelming I have not always chosen to self-harm – sometimes these things work …

Date ……………………………………………

The situation I fear most is…

Date ……………………………………….

My miracle situation would be…

Date ……………………………………………

Elaine Fogarty

When I smile it is because...

Date ....

....
....
....
....
....
....
....
....
....
....
....
....
....
....
....
....

Self-harm, secrets and lies

When I isolate myself and shut down it is because…

Date ....

Elaine Fogarty

When I find a way to engage and enjoy life it is because…

Date ....

I feel most like my true self when…

Date ……………………………………….

Elaine Fogarty

When I look in the mirror I see…

Date ……………………………………….

In my dreams I can allow myself to…

Date ....

Elaine Fogarty

My day has been worthwhile if...

Date ……………………………………………

Self-harm, secrets and lies

I can be really proud of myself for…

Date ………………………………………..

……………………………………………………………….
……………………………………………………………….
……………………………………………………………….
……………………………………………………………….
……………………………………………………………….
……………………………………………………………….
……………………………………………………………….
……………………………………………………………….
……………………………………………………………….
……………………………………………………………….
……………………………………………………………….
……………………………………………………………….
……………………………………………………………….
……………………………………………………………….
……………………………………………………………….

Elaine Fogarty

My perfect day would be...

Date ....

The things I am grateful for are...

Date ……………………………………

Elaine Fogarty

The positive attributes I admire most in others are...

Date ....

....
....
....
....
....
....
....
....
....
....
....
....
....
....
....

Self-harm, secrets and lies

The positive attributes I acknowledge in myself are…

Date ……………………………………………

……………………………………………………
……………………………………………………
……………………………………………………
……………………………………………………
……………………………………………………
……………………………………………………
……………………………………………………
……………………………………………………
……………………………………………………
……………………………………………………
……………………………………………………
……………………………………………………
……………………………………………………
……………………………………………………
……………………………………………………

My thoughts on dealing with challenges and change...

Date ....

The way I could use my skills to help others is…

Date ……………………………………

……………………………………………………
……………………………………………………
……………………………………………………
……………………………………………………
……………………………………………………
……………………………………………………
……………………………………………………
……………………………………………………
……………………………………………………
……………………………………………………
……………………………………………………
……………………………………………………
……………………………………………………
……………………………………………………

Elaine Fogarty

The letter I wish I could send would say…

Date ……………………………………………….

The conversation I wish I could have would be...

Date ………………………………………….

To keep learning I plan to…

Date ……………………………………..

The questions I need to ask the professionals are…

Date ……………………………………..

The things I need to start focussing on are..

Date ....

....
....
....
....
....
....
....
....
....
....
....
....
....
....
....
....

Self-harm, secrets and lies
Who am I ?

Take a moment now to imagine you are looking at a pile of post lying on the ground in your own home. You can see various flyers and promotional leaflets, a catalogue, a group newsletter, two white envelopes with a printed label addressed to Mr or Mrs X, a brown envelope with a label that just says 'The occupier' and a white envelope that is handwritten and addressed to you by your full name - which piece of post will you open first? Most will choose the handwritten envelope and when encouraged to share their reasons why, it usually happens because it looks like 'real' post, something personal. The other post is all for you as well yet you will almost certainly open the envelope that uses your first name or is handwritten because you believe it will contain a message that is only for you, that it represents a connection with the part of you that few see, that it is unique, valued and 'real.'

A pile of post represents some of the roles and responsibilities we have taken on in life and we carry labels all the time - we are mothers, brothers and children - we are students, employees, tenants, customers and members - we are carers, clients, friends and more. There is nothing wrong with this but sometimes we are so busy fulfilling these and other roles that we find ourselves lost and forget the one person at the heart of them all. I invite you in coming days to pause occasionally as you encounter your own labels and consider the person you are when they are stripped away, to remember who you actually are and what you actually need. If you have acquired a label that is misplaced, derogatory or limiting then it is all the more important to look beneath and remember the unique person under there, the person who exists regardless of the judgement of others and does not require their validation to live the life they were meant to live.
Who are you?

Who are you when no one is looking, when you are alone with your thoughts or doing something that makes you truly happy, when no one is asking anything of you? Who are you when the labels are peeled back? Identifying strongly with some of our labels can make us feel good or can drain our self-confidence; our labels are powerful and can in part dictate the path we take in life but self-care requires us to look beyond them. There is no guilt or shame with self-care; when we identify and look after our own needs and stay well then we are better placed to help others and to fulfil our various roles and responsibilities.

The question of who we are is not limited to the minds of famous philosophers but should sit with ease within us all; its exploration is the cornerstone of all wellbeing.

Figure out who you really are and nurture that, you deserve no less.

Self-harm, secrets and lies

Find a picture of your 5 year old self and paste it here.

My younger self

Looking into those eyes…
If I met this child and it needed my help to stay well and safe – how would I feel about that?

....
....
....
....
....

How would I keep it safe?

How would I keep it healthy?

What would I teach it?

How would I nurture it?

How would I like it to see itself?

My younger self

Self-harm, secrets and lies

The 'Me' I am today

Place photo of yourself here

How much of this care can I give to the person in this picture?

....
....
....
....
....
....
....
....
....
....
....
....
....
....
....
....

What is difficult about thinking this way?

....
....
....
....

What is easy about thinking this way?

....
....
....
....

Date ....

A friend tells me that he is feeling overwhelmed by pressures, that he is exhausted and hasn't had time for a relaxed evening meal in weeks. He tells me that his days run into each other and time gets lost, that he works so hard to look after things and tries to help people when he can; he hasn't told anyone else how he is feeling because he doesn't want them to worry – he is convinced the tiredness will pass as it always does and he can get back to his routine.
I care about him. What advice would I give?

....
....
....
....
....
....
....
....

Why I think it is so hard to see what is happening within myself? – to accept the advice that I would so readily give to others?

....
....
....
....
....
....
....

Date ....

My best friend doesn't meet to go shopping anymore – I miss the weekly trip to the gym with them as well. It's always something with them… somewhere to go… something to do… and although I understand all these things are important and they so love being involved, I can't help but wonder when they find time to switch off, if they are even trying anymore to switch off. They always say yes… have forgotten how to say no. They are always smiling but I can see it… something isn't right. What advice would I give?

....
....
....
....
....
....
....
....

Why would it be important for me to take care of myself like this? Is it selfish to practice self-care?

....
....
....
....
....
....
....
....

Date ....

Someone I care about has started acting a little strange lately – they are more quiet, withdrawn. They avoid answering my questions or change the subject when I try to talk about certain things – sometimes they get very defensive or angry and I don't understand why. It's like there is an invisible barrier now between us and I don't know how to breach it. I know they are keeping secrets and I want to respect that but I also fear the secrets are hiding some very real pain. I want to help. I am worried they may be overwhelmed and trying to struggle alone with some serious issues.
I care about them. How would I support them?

....
....
....
....
....
....
....

Why I think it is so difficult to notice changes like this in my own life when they happen?

....
....
....
....
....
....
....

Date ....

What does self-care mean to me?

....
....
....
....
....
....
....
....
....
....
....
....

Why I deserve self-care…

....
....
....
....
....
....
....
....
....

Date ....

Ways in which I could practice self-care are...

....
....
....
....
....
....
....
....
....
....
....
....
....
....
....
....
....
....
....
....
....
....
....
....

Date ....

Things I could start doing right now – TODAY – to take care of myself mentally and physically…

....
....
....
....
....
....
....
....
....
....
....
....
....
....
....
....
....
....
....
....
....
....
....

The 28 day Self-care challenge

Introducing new habits into our lives can be challenging and so often people feel that they have failed when it just doesn't 'click in'

This is often a matter of simple timing.

For a newly introduced idea or action to become habit and have any chance of daily sustainability it requires at least 28 days of repeated practice. If you can do it or think it consistently in the same way with the same level of enthusiasm and effort every single day for those 28 days then you are far more likely to see it take hold and become a normal part of your life.

Use the following chart to record your Self-care practice for 28 days.
Do at least one thing EVERY single day. Claim your time EVERY single day.
This is not a test of willpower it is a positive exploration. Should you have need to self-harm during these 28 days you have NOT failed – do NOT stop. Keep going!

Self-harm, secrets and lies

Start date ....

Day 1 ....

Day 2 ....

Day 3 ....

Day 4 ....

Day 5 ....

Day 6 ....

Day 7 ....

Day 8 ....

You're doing well – keep it up

Day 9 ....

Day 10 ....

Day 11 ....

Day 12 ....

Day 13 ....

Day 14 ....

Day 15 ....

Day 16 ....

Day 17 ....

Day 18 ....

Day 19 …………………………………………

Day 20 …………………………………………

Day 21 …………………………………………

Three weeks in – Almost there – You are creating a new you – Keep going

Day 22 …………………………………………

Day 23 …………………………………………

Day 24 …………………………………………

Day 25 …………………………………………

Day 26 …………………………………………

Day 27 …………………………………………

Just one more day to go

Day 28
....

✎ My thoughts on Self-care now

Author's Perspective

Content may be a possible trigger.

There follows a selection of genuine unedited journal entries and sketches spanning many years - offered to give perspective, prompt personal enquiry and helpful conversations.

Elaine Fogarty

The blade

I can't post a photo but wish you could see,
The scars on my arm that are calling to me.
I'm so overwhelmed I can barely breathe,
I need my blade to make it all leave.

I close my eyes but see them still,
Fresh cuts, deep cuts; my thoughts they fill.
It all makes sense. I know it's right
Yet I somehow resist, and reclaim my night.

It's hard to deny what you know to be true,
To convince yourself to think it all through.
It's hard to move on and find other ways,
To ignore the blade and the things it says.

I can't explain it but I wish you could know,
How it feels to be me and need the blade so.
The sting of the cut, the blood that flows,
The smile it raises, the peace it bestows.

Release

Mall-adaptive, ill-advised, and many other things … yet despite knowing all this and having almost abandoned it, today I found myself returning to a coping mechanism that I could be sure of. One by one I laid out about me all parts of the ritual and welcomed back an old friend. A silent embrace. Assistance without condition. Emotional release. The longed for nothingness palpable in every breath. I knew it wouldn't last… but then I was also sure I wouldn't last without it. Somewhere deep inside I caught a glimpse of myself standing in warm sun; for a time my old friend chased away the darkness

Self-harm, secrets and lies
Just a conversation

I just packed everything away again - and yet again there is a dressing on my arm. I hate that I did it and I hate that it felt like the only way to cope. I had taken as much medication as I safely could but could just not calm the sense of panic and loss. I felt abandoned. (...) has left now - the conversation is over. I feel betrayed and quite adrift in a life that suddenly makes no sense. I did what I needed to do and now between those cuts and those unspoken words I feel even more useless and unloved. (...) I can't talk about it and may never talk about it...)
It hurts so bad. At least for a while though blood can take the edge off.

Elaine Fogarty

Clouds

Depression brings many challenges - one of the most troublesome for me at the minute is the increase in thoughts of self-harm. My mind does not linger too long and as yet I have managed the thoughts by treating them like clouds in the sky - I see them - I may even pause to consider the shapes they form in my mind, but I let them pass. Clouds drift across the sky and confused and overlapping images such as these drift across my mind - as yet there is no rain - I see them pass and observe form give way to shifting abstract - I see them pass and with each one passes the moment. These are the images I see but they are phantoms conjured to pull me into the darkness and I have no wish to go further. Thoughts such as these invade my mind and challenge me to respond but I have not - I am determined to weather the storm - I remind myself that self-harm is not the only coping tool available to me. I remind myself that there is no need to be scared. I remind myself that there is always choice. I remind myself that I am not my thoughts - I am simply ME.

3 Things

There are 3 things you really need to know about if you are considering taking away the tools I use to harm myself. Whether you approve or understand them makes no difference – the truth is what it is. Before you judge me, before you make assumptions about my circumstances, you need to stop and consider..................

Taking away my tools probably won't stop me. I will find others and hide them better.
You may cause even worse self-harm because I will be driven to use tools or methods that are less safe and way

less hygienic and I will act in desperation rather than with the measure of ritual and control I normally do.

You may drive me into a full crisis. No matter how good your intentions, you may actually be taking away my last remaining coping mechanism – the one thing between me and falling apart completely, perhaps even a crisis of suicidal intent.

And the 4th third thing – there is ALWAYS another way.

Elusive Explanations

When folk look at me with pity – I wish I could explain.
When eyes burn with condemnation – I wish I could explain.
When soft voices try to fix me – I wish I could explain.
They see me as vulnerable, as troubled, as sick, as bad,
But I'm actually the strong one.
I wish I could explain but a simple tenth of the challenges I've come through.

Power

Sometimes I like to mentally dismantle and dissect my surroundings in an exercise of preparedness. Knowing me and my history some would look around the same space and congratulate themselves on identifying the objects I could use to self-harm or make a suicide attempt, but for every 5 they can think of I've already thought of 15 and I have stored them away with mental note of possible effectiveness and ease of access. For every obvious thing they remove I have experience enough still find what I need in at least 5 other places, often hidden in plain sight. There is no such thing as a totally "safe" environment – trying to remove all possible points of self-harm is like trying to stop the tide by removing a few buckets of water. The only safety comes from inside my own mind and if people really want to help that is where the point of intervention lies. Leave a paring knife lying on the bench and yes, I may take it and use it but leave the thought of hope in my mind and I may quicker take that. Objects don't hold the power – thoughts do. Encourage, educate and empower. Support me in making my own decisions and accept they are truly mine to make.

Self-harm, secrets and lies

Sad

It's a sad thing indeed,
To live in fear of your own mind,
To swim against the current
Of rushing thoughts,
To struggle,
To tire,
To slip beneath the surface.

The edge

The sense of life, invisible,
Hangs upon a blade,
The balance of life, untenable,
Until the cut is made.
The future of life, unknowable,
And yet simple plans are laid

Enough

And then,
The morning came,
And with it gratitude for the strand that held when
Others fell away.
The morning came,
And that should be enough.

.

Elaine Fogarty

Truth

Wonderful, spontaneous, life-defining clarity,
Loud and effervescent...
Vibrant and bright...
Clears not the path, but shines forth a light

Places

I burn or cut in all the usually 'non-public' places – shoulders, thighs, chest, abdomen, and feet. My preferred place has always been my lower left arm and that is definitely open to public judgement. My acts of self-harm are driven by either a need for control or a need for release and both of these can now be satisfied by relatively small shallow wounds. My practice has evolved and the statement made is qualified with a measure of self-care.

I self-treat and I am careful that most of my wounds now heal with little or no additional scarring. However, crucially, I need the existing scars – they have emotional currency, they bear witness to my journey and my survival. I NEED them. I have accepted them and no longer hide them from the world. They are important to me. Even in times of crisis past where the need to have fresh injury has been overwhelming I have cut carefully over the top of existing scars – I haven't wished to spoil a perfect canvas. Even when I got a tattoo to celebrate my personal survival and personal responsibility I had the artist carefully avoid covering any of the scars on my lower arm and instead nestle the little butterfly amongst them.

Do not misunderstand – my scars are not a means to attract attention but rather they simply exist – they are what they are and there is no apology offered. We are happy my scars and I to entertain enquiry for we have much to teach a judgemental world, but mostly we find the internal dialogue much sweeter. Time does not lessen that.

Sharing

Sometimes I join conversations in online Forum or even just pop in to answer a few queries or share some coping tools. I blend in. I feel welcome. The people I encounter there accept me as a peer, and there is no need of personal sharing beyond the experience. Occasionally though the topic drives inevitably towards the question… How old are you?

Perhaps they pick up on the fact that my narratives do not centre around school life with parents or the struggle to hide evidence and tools. They ask and I answer 49.

Their struggle to assimilate that information is for a brief moment palpable, even online. Two main issues arise from this revelation – the questions around how young I was when I started and how I hadn't found a way to completely stop in all that time.

Now and then I am blessed to be able to share some of my personal recovery story and let people know that self-harm can be managed. I do not lie. I do still turn to self-harm in circumstances of overwhelm where I feel trapped and scared – not always – but sometimes – as a last resort. My message is that we each have in us the strength to find and use other tools. Harming does not make us bad people. Harming does not have to dictate our path in life.

I'm no different

Would you ask and alcoholic why he is addicted to alcohol? Would you ask a drug addict why she is driven to use? Can a smoker be expected to fully explain the mechanisms that power his cravings? All of these people can answer is that their substance of choice serves a purpose, addresses a deep and powerful need, a voice that simply must be silenced. I am no different. I may never identify the point at which my chosen behaviour morphed into an addiction. In terms of my general mental health I talk now about being in recovery – in terms of self-harm I remain a recovering addict. I see no shame in that.

Self-harm, secrets and lies

Hiding

We mostly hide our scars and evidence of fresh activity – we who self-harm live by deceit. There are many places on the body to actively purge the pain safe in the knowledge that clothing will cover them and most of the time we get away with it. Some of us though are conflicted because we have a need to see the marks and to watch them heal (or prevent them from healing) and for us there is need to be creative. People are so used now to seeing sports supports on wrists, knees ankles etc. that these can be employed when going out in public and indeed the cut to size tubular compression bandages area godsend for concealment without query. People will accept these quicker than the wearing of say, long sleeves in summer or trousers at an event where dresses are the norm. Well placed chunky jewellery is great way to distract the eye and temporary tattoos can work wonders. These and other tricks keep the judgemental questioning at bay and help protect us by forming a 'bubble' of normality for public hours. We keep secrets not to hurt others but to keep ourselves safe in the face of forces we don't always fully understand. Hiding is sometimes a necessity and lies reinforce that. It can be hard to move past the need.

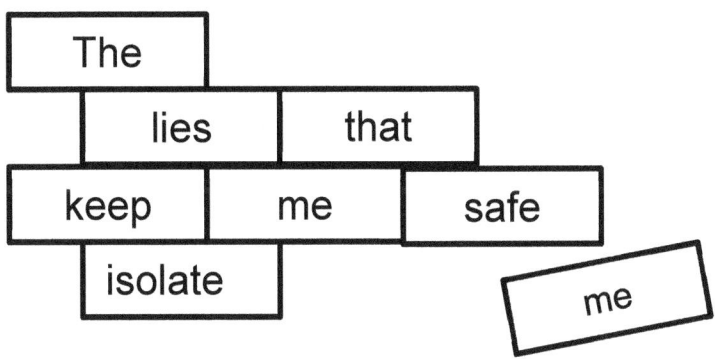

Elaine Fogarty

Lost

My limited vocabulary
Will not permit expression.
I grope aimlessly for words
But they simply are not there.
I feel agitated, no, restless;
Something isn't right.
I've lost myself,
Yet am here to witness the loss.
Questions go unanswered.
Thoughts scramble to understand.
They are swallowed up by the void,
And reason itself deserts me.

She

The girl in the mirror disgusts me;
She is the truth of me,
She is failure incarnate.

Box, Blade, Drive, Blood and Benediction

Logic is not so comforting right now when it is being drowned out by the voices in my head – the chorus of my self-deprecating judgemental shattered self. Comfort food is not so comforting when it sits in my stomach like lead and coats my tongue with foul fake flavours. Comfort food is not so comforting when sugars dash straight to my head and begin to race around and around – my head holds attention with all the suspense of a pressure vessel that is about to explode. It has happened before. It will happen again – the sugar rush is going to trample the meds into the ground and mock them as it over-rides every attempt at sleep. All of this and not only do I find myself without comfort, I find myself without self-respect. How could I do this to myself? I feel sick. I feel weak. I feel like reaching for the key for the box for the only remaining solution. I so need my blade because things make sense when I hold it, things make sense when I use it, things make sense as the healing starts. Beneath the scars is where I have lived most of my life and I can barely contain the urge to nestle back in there. I haven't held that key for quite a while but part of me is driven to go pull it from it's hiding place – I need to feel the feelings that only my blade can release – perhaps I have locked them away too long - Box, Blade, Basic drive, Blood and Benediction. Can I make it to morning? Can I find another way?

Terminator style perspective

When you take an honest look at yourself and the self-harm looks back it can be difficult to accept. In time identity settles and perspective settles – it becomes normal… not normal enough to make you feel you can talk about it with others, but a strange kind of normal that is almost comforting. A little more time goes by and it becomes a need, perhaps even a compulsion and when you need that comfort you find its promise in every object, every situation – it is literally everywhere you look.

In the Terminator films the camera allows us to see the writing scroll across his field of vision, superimposing the information he needed. Sometimes I feel a little like that is happening to me. When my self-harm urges are overwhelming I look around me and almost every item I scan has information on how to use it for self-harm. It is weird – normal for me but weird I guess in the 'real' world. I know I can see way past the obvious uses for things and I will always find something – even in a room that others believe

Elaine Fogarty

is safe. My Terminator style perspective means I am never more than a few feet away from the tools I need.

I could illustrate this better if I gave actual examples but there are two very good reasons why that isn't going to happen...

1 – I won't put others at risk by offering ideas or creating triggers

2 – I am not about to give up my secrets, I may not need them at the minute but still, I will not surrender my secrets.

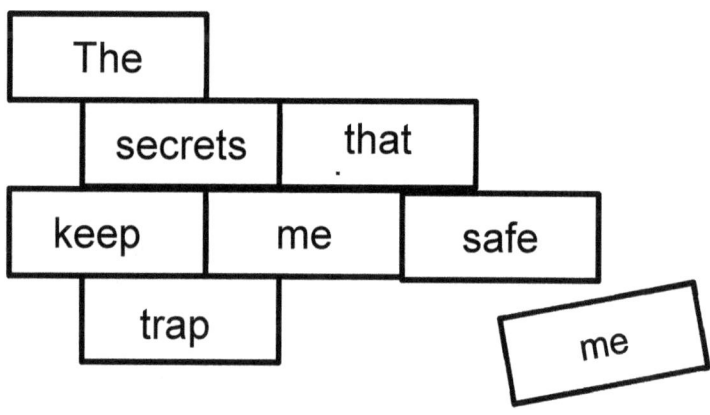

The hunt

Guilt, like many carnivores,
Hunts in the broad light of day.
Quiet and unnoticed,
It sleeps through the night,
Arising with the sun to prey.
Carefully stalking,
With a hunger unending,
It hunts upon the stray

Self-harm, secrets and lies

The dance

So I tugged the sleeve down even lower,
And smiled an awkward smile,
Unashamed of cuts and scars and scratches,
Yet I hid them for a while.
I hid them for my peers and friends,
Lest I trigger equal pain,
Yet they danced beneath the fabric,
Demanding air again.
Their likeness danced around my mind,
As sensation set the tune.
Unashamed of cuts and scars and scratches,
Meeting's end came not too soon.

Tattoo

Today,
I have this little butterfly.
It rests upon my arm.
It quietly reminds me
To resist self-harm.
Tomorrow
Weakness may just kill it,
But today it lives in hope.
My little temporary tattoo,
Simply helps me cope.
Right now,
I don't care if you see it.
I don't care if you ask.
I'm so tired of hiding illness;
So sick of wearing masks.

Elaine Fogarty

Flight

Miles do not true distance make,
For pain has wings to soar,
To hang a time amongst the clouds,
Then come home to roost once more.

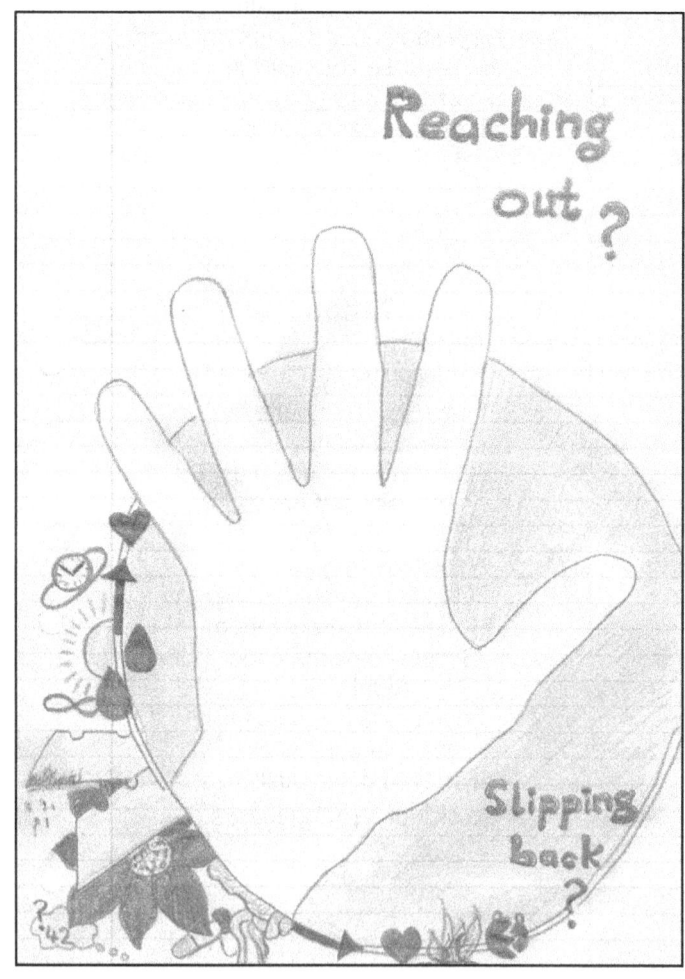

Self-harm, secrets and lies

Whisper

"There is a constant stinging sensation coming from my arm. There is no pain, just this whisper reminding me of recent cuts. I won't go into detail because it would be unfair to risk triggering someone else, but it is what it is ... I cut ... and somehow it made everything seem a little better, as it always does. I'm going into work soon and I've chosen to wear a long sleeved top – it gives me options – three inch square white dressings are not easy to conceal but then they know about my 'issues' in work which means I shouldn't have to worry about covering up on such a warm and clammy day. I guess I'll play it by ear when I get in. It's going to be a very long day in work today because I am genuinely in no state to get anything done – my mind will not be on the job at hand, that's for sure... But in I go because I'm thinking it's better than sitting the eight hours alone with my thoughts"

If they ask...

"My arm has 'marks' on it at the moment – some permanent scars and some healing areas where the skin had been scratched raw; I don't think it looks that bad, it's been a lot worse. I very rarely hide my arms away any more because I'm no longer ashamed of them. I don't wear my 'marks' as a badge of honour announcing allegiance to some misunderstood sub-culture, but I simply allow them to exist. If people see them they see them. If people ask I answer. It is what it is. My self-harm is mild on a comparative scale, but still difficult to explain sometimes: today I had to find a succinct way to do it for someone close who was totally unaware of my mental illness and who was using English as her second language. A challenge. It was a few hours ago but if I recall correctly I simply responded to her pointing finger and puzzled query with this... "Oh, no ... it's not that ... I did it myself ... How can I explain? ... Did he tell you about my illness, my mental illness? Well sometimes people who are sick like that, they do this...they self-harm... I did this... I self-harm too." I needn't have worried – her hug told me she understood."

Elaine Fogarty

Blades

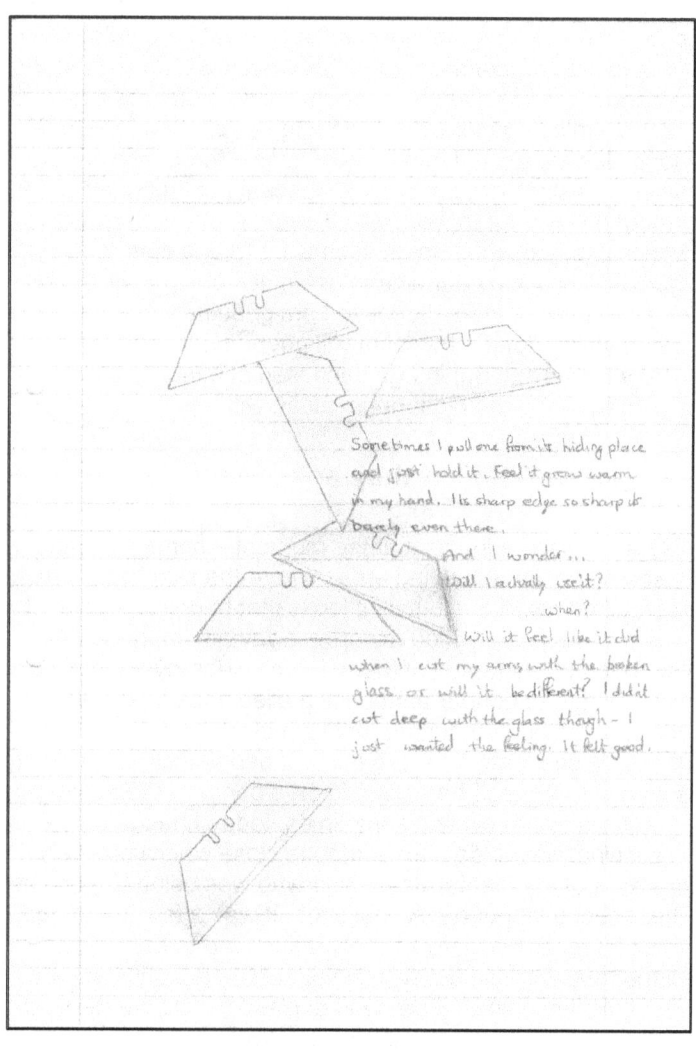

Sometimes I pull one from its hiding place and just hold it. Feel it grow warm in my hand. Its sharp edge so sharp it barely even there.

And I wonder...
Will I actually use it?
...when?
Will it feel like it did when I cut my arms with the broken glass, or will it be different? I didn't cut deep with the glass though - I just wanted the feeling. It felt good.

Self-harm, secrets and lies

140-3
The butterfly is fading, the lines below it too, but cutting works so very well –
What else is there to do?

140-4
I only have fine scars; I never cut that deep, but I have dark and detailed plans,
and secrets still to keep.

140-13
Just because they're shallow, doesn't mean there is less pain.
Just because they're hidden, doesn't mean she's safe again.

Challenging a self-harm trigger

"Dark thoughts often come uninvited, but occasionally they arrive when the door is left ajar by an innocent word, smell, object – trigger. Today, in fact for many days now, I've been doing great. I feel about as stable as I ever get to feel and life seems less of a personal challenge. Things are good. This afternoon though, one of those split-second, ambush-you-from-out-of-nowhere triggers came at me – screamed so loud at me that I just couldn't ignore it. It got inside my head and resurrected a bundle of feelings so jumbled that I almost caught myself panic. A few shards of broken glass resting on a carpeted cutting bench. That's all. They had no doubt been there since the picture framing department closed over a year ago and as the room was now little more than a corridor to other places, what need had there ever been to sweep them up? They were harmless. I was easily 12 feet away but I could clearly see the sharp edges of the clustered pieces contrasted against that dirty brown – in fact, for a moment, it was all I could see. How could I not have noticed them before? Memories of previous cuts came rushing at me with an intensity I had not expected and the trigger lived up to its name. All of a sudden, my head was full of images best not described here in detail; my mind was besieged by thoughts trying to justify them. In that split second I found myself wanting to cut again – I so wanted to. But, to my credit, I turned 90 degrees and headed for the double doors and down into the warehouse. I walked its length slowly and then took a detour outside through the loading bays, all the while trying to regain my composure. By the time I walked back into the offices I was ok and my afternoon continued as if nothing had ever happened. It does happen though. More often than you would think. I can't control the triggers but I'm trying to control how I deal with them. Just another day as me."

Dreams

Last night was interrupted by really bad dreams – all about cutting myself badly, lots of blood. The images were so clear. I kept waking feeling really upset, and then I'd sleep, dream badly and wake again. Blood, lots of blood. Mine I think but I never saw myself – just the blood. Pools of gloopy thick dark red and sploshes and splats of finer stuff.
On waking I couldn't remember how or why but I remember the blood wouldn't stop – weird. I found my hand drawn to the itch of recent scarring and as I massaged the area it somehow eased the discomfort. I looked down to check it was really closed and healing for it became the focus for all the imagery. Suddenly it all made sense.
I'd been in denial about how serious my problems were and without once lifting a blade I felt them break apart and float fragmented in the imagined bloody pools.
Imagined wounds. Imagined healing. Very real results.

Self-harm, secrets and lies

It's 3.54 in the morning and as usual I can't sleep.
Different thoughts tonight.
I'm remembering the last time I cut myself – how it felt, wondering where would be the best place to do it again where it wouldn't be seen, wondering what to use.
I try to divert my thoughts but all that comes to mind is a scene from a film I once saw where a girl cuts quite extensively and the graphic detail floods my mind. A rush of emotion and sudden need to lift the blade in front of me is all-consuming. Certain knowledge of blood red peace fills my every thought and I must have it. I see my inviting bare thigh and I wonder… What would it matter anyway? Who would

know? Why should I let their judgement drive me? I need what I need. The mental assault that pierces my night is unrelenting – it must stop. At least for a while I'd feel release.
Silence. Warmth. Smiles. The falling away of weight I was never designed to carry.

Giving up

I understand now that a need to scratch my skin to bleeding or burn or cut is all about learned patterns. I don't know when my brain made the connection but it did and I now live with the truth of it – self-harm equals release, equals control in a life stubbornly out of my control. I'm careful and I work as safely as I can but I'm still left with scars. The process of healing and the presence of those scars are themselves strangely therapeutic but underneath it all I hear the whisper that it is self-destructive and that I should break free of the patterns. I need to find another way.

Tonight I gathered the last of my secret stash of pristine blades and wrapped them carefully in bubble wrap and slotted them into a postal bag – for purely symbolic reasons I am posting them to some friends along with a letter that breaks the silence. I feel sad. I feel glad. I feel scared. I've never really talked about my blades before, let alone given them up. I'm realistic enough to know this will not magically fix anything but I am trying to test the waters, test my dependence, and test my options. I want to believe I can use the breathing space to find some other tools. Surely there are other ways to deal with pain and overwhelm. If I can let go of these them perhaps some of the pictures and plans will leave with them? I need to believe I can make progress and reclaim control in a safer way.

I gathered them from all the places I had hidden them and surprised myself with how many I ended up with – 1 from my

Self-harm, secrets and lies

coat, 2 from my handbag, 1 from under the mattress, 1 from behind the picture frame, 1 from under the carpet in the bedroom, 3 from inside a tampon box, 1 inside a book. Only a few of these were hygienically stored as coping tools and the others I slowly conceded were hidden for ease of access in suicidal crisis. The realisation that the lines were blurring was scary and I needed the blades gone so that I had space to think without them calling to me.

I've reached a pivotal point in my life – next week I am going voluntarily on to a psychiatric ward for observation and hopefully get some insight into the mess my mind has become. Control was an illusion and I'm done lying to myself. I need help and it starts here. I'm a little panicky but I think I'm doing the right thing. I've been in the darkness before but this time I feel without purpose. I feel lost. Nothing makes sense and that is a dangerous way to be feeling when surrounded by blades. I need to distance myself for a while and take the terrifying step of trusting some strangers to help me make sense of things.

Yes it is purely symbolic and yes I could buy more blades in the corner shop almost on whim, I could go to the kitchen and grab a knife, I could break a lightbulb or dismantle a sharpener…… there are so many other easy ways to draw blood but I'm letting go of the main tools and hoping the time on the ward will allow me to move past the very real addiction of their use.

If I ever hold a blade again at least I would hope to be able to do so as a rare and considered act rather than have it hold me.

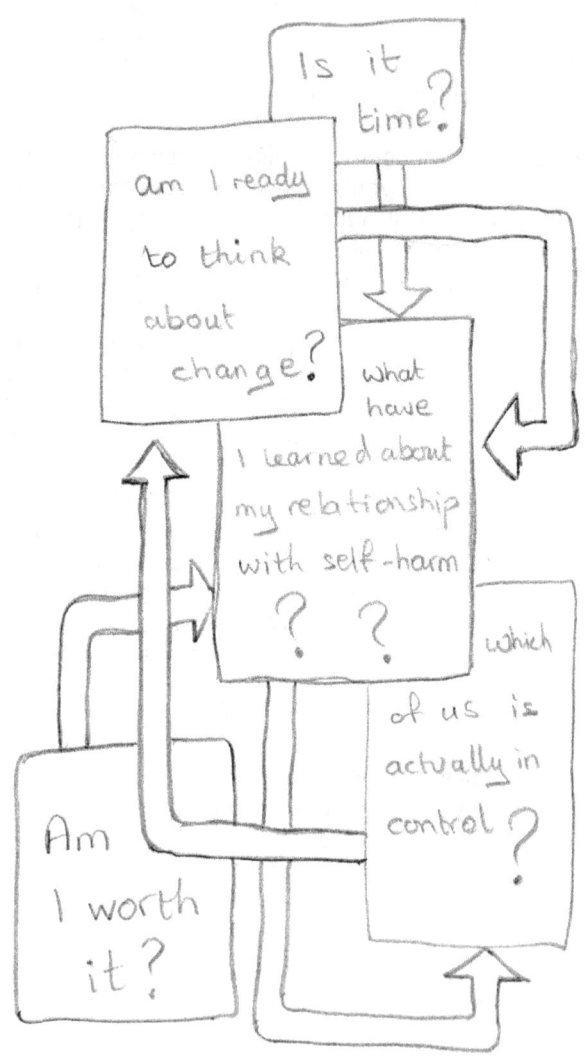

Self-harm, secrets and lies

Returning Whispers

No smile tonight. I feel uncomfortable and upset with myself. Why can't I make these thoughts just go away? I hear myself weigh up the reasons why blood could help but instantly recoil – tears flow and my hand shakes. Where is my usual lullaby? I feel desperate and betrayed. I can hardly breathe for the thoughts themselves fill the space around me and squeeze the air from my lungs. It has worked so many times before and it should work now... I don't understand. I grow angry and then in that anger find the strength to push through. It will work. I will make it work. I cut deep.
It does.
I lie back and float in the resulting haze, high on the best sensations my blade has ever brought me. I'm home – nobody and nothing can touch me here. It's finally gone, all of it. I'm free. I cleanse and dress the wound with paper stitches and then cover up with clothes; no one need ever know the origin of my resilience.

Recovering addict

Self-harm is a highly addictive behaviour and like all addictions it claims you piece by piece; it makes promises and skilfully offers us choice. We are of course free to make those choices but we are never free of the consequences of them... I accepted long ago that I would have to live my life with my illness but I never factored in living under the shadow of a self-imposed addiction. My choices. My consequences. It is still difficult for me though, now that I am in mental health recovery, to find that some aspects of my daily struggles are beyond the comprehension or the emotional capacity of people around me – it can get very lonely and sometimes very frustrating. The self-harm issues sometimes cause more problems than the general mental health issues that gave birth to them.

Elaine Fogarty

If I were a recovering alcoholic everyone would I am sure understand if I chose not to take a job working bar in an Ibiza nightclub – too many memories, too many temptations, too many triggers, too much risk. Because my temptations and triggers and risk lie all round me in common household objects, I live my life with that kind of exposure and challenge all the time but no-one offers the same understanding.

Sometimes individual triggers rise up to taunt me in the most public way and I want so to act on them. Sometimes individual triggers rise up to taunt me and I struggle to hold myself together just long enough to find a quiet private place to act on them… I never know which way it will go. One day a blade will just be a blade, a flame a flame, and another it will be the psiron that lures me to my dark and conflicted fate.

It took a long time to be comfortable saying the words
"I have a mental illness"
It took even longer to come to terms with
"I'm a recovering addict."

This one image shows the two coping tools I have found most helpful in dealing with my own self-harm issues over the past few years.

The beaded bracelet is a mala used in meditation, a skill that has woven itself into my everyday life and made many things possible.

Self-harm, secrets and lies

The butterfly is a tattoo but for many years it was preceded by temporary versions as a self-harm 'time buying' tool. This is a very popular and effective technique.

When the urge arises to self-harm you draw with non-permanent marker or place a temporary tattoo in the area where you are drawn to act out the urge. For many of this it is the forearm or wrist but it can be anywhere. Then you simply commit to not actually harming until that butterfly,

however formed, wears away of its own accord. This works really well and stems from 'The butterfly project' as widely discussed online. Males can use the technique too but they must be creative and choose imagery that it is suitable. My transition to a permanent version was not taken lightly but it was definitely the right choice for me.

Another benefit of this technique is that it allow us to discreetly identify others who share our challenges and if appropriate engage in conversation and mutual support; sometimes even the silent exchange of acknowledging glances is enough to shatter that day's crushing isolation.

For the most part it has been an insider thing, part of the peer lexicon that professionals cannot understand but there is a growing acceptance and even encouraged use now by some of those same professionals. This technique is not age limited and indeed works very well in what would be considered one of the biggest areas of incidence – young teenage girls. It has worked for my 49 year old and my 13 year old selves equally and not many coping mechanisms offer that breadth of range. I would recommend it as both one who self-harms and a therapist.

Elaine Fogarty

Elaine Fogarty

This is the chapter of the book that almost didn't get written – the one that almost fell foul of societal judgement before it was even committed to paper. The subject of offering guidance or comment on safe practice to those who self-harm is highly controversial because many, including some families and some professionals, believe it is at best counter-productive and at worst simply provides a blueprint for how to start, continue and expand the practice.

As someone who has lived experience of self-harm, I could not write a book about the subject and leave it out. If it attracts disapproval then that is unfortunate but I genuinely believe it necessary – safe practice can help manage the urges and it can save lives.

This book does not encourage the practice of self-harm but it acknowledges the role it plays for many as a coping tool – there are lots of other excellent ways to deal with issues and by working your way through this book you have already begun your exploration these alternatives to physical harm. Safe practice is as much about that transition as anything else and it begins with understanding your own needs. Gradual introduction of better, cleaner, safer, equally effective tools is also safe practice… this is a positive thing to harness but do not lose sight of your goal to stop.

One wouldn't learn to drive a car without first learning how to use the brakes properly and do an emergency stop, so let's apply the same principal and recap on to the issue of self-treatment and recognition of intervention points for emergency care.

Self-harm, secrets and lies

When to seek emergency care after self-harming

…Seek help if…

You have taken an overdose
You have ingested a poison
Your breathing is compromised
You have severe chest pain
Blood is spurting from the wound
Your tool breaks and part becomes lodged inside a wound
You have cut deep enough to expose muscle
You have a burn on somewhere sensitive like face, palm or a joint
You have a chemical burn of any kind
You have in any way damaged the eyes
You have bleeding which won't stop
You have loss of sensation around the area of harm
You have loss of sensation anywhere else
You have cold clammy skin, persistent dizziness or rapid pulse
Your wound or burn is larger than 6cm in size

You notice days later any swelling, weeping, foul smell or aching
(Any of these may be sign of an infection)

Elaine Fogarty

What to expect from a visit to the hospital emergency department

If your self-harm brings you to the Emergency room of your local hospital it can be a difficult and emotionally charged situation for all involved. Hospital staff are people too, and although professionally trained, some will have difficulty understanding the issues around self-harm so good communication on both sides will be vital.

You will be in the right place to get the help you need.

You will need to calmly answer a lot of questions about what you have done, how you did it, the substances involved, times, amounts, names, history etc. but although this may seem unnecessary and annoying it is very important. You will be asked about allergies, medications, and current medical issues and yes – almost certainly someone will ask why you did what you did. The motive behind this cannot be assumed to be negative or derogatory as while gathering history they will also be trying to make an early assessment of your mental state to make sure you stay safe.

A professional with specific mental health training may have a more detailed conversation with you and ask about your motives, your history of self-harm, and your plans around hurting yourself. There may be a temptation here to react with anger or to lie but honesty will secure you the best possible help so you should take the opportunity to speak freely. It is a challenging environment but the staff you encounter should be fully trained and focused on providing the best possible care. Depending on the nature of your self-harm you may have treatment and be sent home relatively quickly or be kept in hospital for other procedures – these may include things like drips, activated charcoal ingestion or having the stomach cleared but there may also follow a more detailed psychiatric assessment. Sometimes an

Self-harm, secrets and lies

appointment with a Mental Health team will made and you will be allowed to go home but if this happens it is very important that you do attend – even if feeling somewhat better. If your assessment warrants further observation it is possible you may be admitted into hospital to facilitate that – again, you will be in the right place to get the best possible care. Staff will answer any questions you have and there will be literature available for you and your family too if appropriate that will explain the process of care ahead. You will also be given information on a wide range of other services that can help you.

If you find yourself caught in a repeating cycle of presenting at hospital with injuries, receiving treatment and going home soon afterwards it may get frustrating. Remember – there is help available and you can speak with hospital staff, your GP, Counsellor, Keyworker or crisis helpline at any time.

You will not be left alone to cope if you directly ask for help

Elaine Fogarty

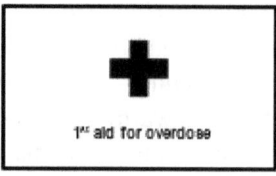

1st aid for overdose

Overdose may be by Ingestion, Injection, Absorption or Inhalation and symptoms may include
Upper abdominal pain or Tenderness – Vomiting or Nausea – Breathing difficulties – Confusion – Delirium – Extreme sleepiness – Slow shallow pulse – Headache – Tremor – Sweating – Hallucinations – Hyperactivity – Shallow breathing

DO NOT
Induce vomiting / eat / drink
Settle to sleep / drive
Try to counteract symptoms by taking other drugs
Ignore need for emergency services based on lack of symptoms

DO
Seek <u>immediate</u> emergency help – time can be of the essence
Be completely honest when speaking with attending staff
Tell attending staff what and how much you've taken (if known)
Hand attending staff the containers and foils you have
Report all new sensations/symptoms
(Leave interpretation to staff)

Self-harm, secrets and lies

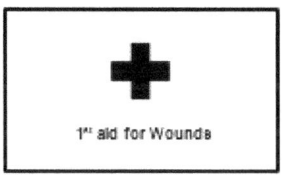

1st aid for Wounds

This term can include Incisions, Lacerations, Abrasions or Punctures. Self-treatment may not always be possible; it is important to remember – if in doubt seek help.

Capillary bleeding will ooze slowly, Arterial bleeding will spurt in time with the heartbeat and venous bleeding will be thick, darker in colour and less pressured with less dramatic flow

DO NOT
Touch the wound itself if at all possible
Try to remove anything that has become lodged inside
Wait too long for bleeding under your applied pressure to stop – seek help if persists
Remove wound-closure strips earlier than 1 week after application

DO
Rinse with running water or clean with an antiseptic wipe or spray
Pat dry with a piece of gauze or improvise with clean kitchen roll
Apply pressure/elevate until bleeding stops
Apply wound closure strips if necessary to pull the edges in close
Use non-adhesive dressing and micro-pore tape to cover the affected area
Change dressing every 2-3 days and monitor closely for signs of infection

Elaine Fogarty

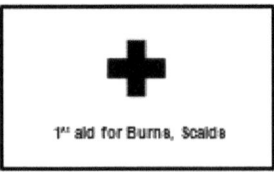

1st aid for Burns, Scalds

Burns may be from Flame, Friction, and Branding/Cigarette for example and scalds may be by Steam, Hot liquids or Hot fats. Chemical burns may be by a wide range of home or industrial liquids, gels or powders.

DO NOT
Touch the affected area if at all possible
Attempt to neutralise acid/alkali burns
Apply lotions, ointments, spays or fat to the burn
Apply any adhesives – choose dressings carefully
Cover or apply pressure with a loose fibre/fluffy product
Remove anything that is sticking to the burn
Cover burns to the face or head – seek help immediately

DO
Seek help <u>immediately</u> if something is stuck to or lodged in the burn
Seek help <u>immediately</u> if the burn area is on a delicate area or is very large
Cool by rinsing for 15-20 mins with cool clean water
Remove watches, jewellery etc. from the nearby areas
Use non-adhesive dressing to cover if available

If the burn requires professional care, wrap in cling film or put a clean plastic bag around area and secure with tape further along to protect it in transit to hospital.

Self-harm, secrets and lies

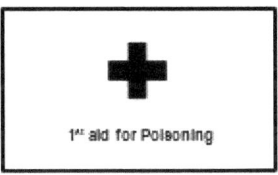

1st aid for Poisoning

DO NOT
Attempt to induce vomiting
Do not attempt to neutralise poison by ingesting another substance
Eat / Drink anything until professional help is available

DO
Seek help immediately
Inform attending staff of details of poison taken, the amount and timescale
Lightly moisten lips frequently with water if irritated but do not drink

Please remember

1st aid information offered in this book is for guidance only.
It is not offered by virtue of any specific medical training.
To make sure you have the most up to date and accurate information
Please make your own regular and careful checks.
If in doubt, seek advice from a trusted source such as The NHS or St. John's Ambulance or Community & workplace training.

Elaine Fogarty

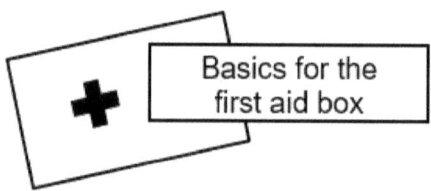

In a watertight box keep a minimum of…

Scissors

Plasters (Individually wrapped)

Non-Adhesive dressing pads (Individually wrapped)

Surgical tape

Clean gauze

Antiseptic wipes or spray

Wound closure strips

Standard bandages

Saline water

Gloves

2 doses of painkiller

Also keep to hand…

Kitchen roll

Cling film

Selection and hygiene for self-harm tools & Safe use

Your goal is to work towards stopping the self-harm. Stay safe as you do so.
If you self-harm by cutting or scratching frequently you may wish to maintain your tetanus injections to help protect you, however best protection is always to choose your tools well and keep them clean. Breaking household items to get sharp edges or randomly using implements you find at hand when the urge strikes is not ideal; toolbox items from the garage even less so. One solution for someone who practices self-harm is actually to create two kits – a first aid kit and a tool kit. By doing this you are protecting yourself on both fronts and you will also have a greater sense of control over your situation as you progress towards diminished use and finally leaving the practice behind. Safety has to be your first priority and you need to plan ahead in order to stay safe but be aware others may not fully understand your intentions around this safety planning

Examine your urges, your patterns, your triggers and your needs so that with each incident you learn more and can make changes towards your goal of stopping; the drive to harm is powerful but you can reclaim some measure of control and keep yourself safe as you in time achieve the same results in better, safer ways. Before you use your tool kit ALWAYS have your 1st aid kit to hand.

Buy or source bladed tools or single blades from trusted places and use <u>only</u> once. Many blades can actually be purchased in sterile wrapping or plastic safety boxes that protect them. Choose sharp tools that will work easily rather than settle for dull or ragged ones which have higher risk of harbouring dirt or causing further unintended harm. If you use syringes keep to single use options. If you use items to cause abrasion on the skin try to ensure they are clean and in a state to work effectively. Keep items well covered inside your actual tool box so that there is less risk of contamination. If you are going to use off the shelf products to damage the skin select those that are single use because the accumulation of skin and other debris would be an infection hazard. With burning or cutting you will also need to understand the nature of scarring and develop a working knowledge around the causes and worsening of skin marks. Certain areas will not only produce worse scars but there is risk of permanent damage and reduced range of movement. You will also need to develop a working knowledge of basic anatomy, knowing where and how there is risk damaging nerves, ligaments, tendons or muscle and how to avoid extreme blood loss or the danger of severing an artery. It can be extremely easy to cut deeper than intended so having the 1st aid kit and emergency numbers to hand is always a sensible precaution,

It is never wise to use overdose of any kind as a means to self-harm even if the aim is just to get attention or to 'zone out' for a while. **THERE IS NO SUCH THING AS A SAFE OVERDOSE.** The varying factors at play around overdose make it a dangerous tool to use and control is an illusion. Stay safe by never stockpiling/specially purchasing extra medication.

Basically safe practice boils down to a few simple questions…

What has my most recent incident of self-harm taught me? Is there an alternative? Is there something safer I could try first? Is this tool fit for purpose? Is it really clean? Do I know how to use it properly? Can I care for the area of harm afterwards?

Self-harm, secrets and lies
Don't make it – Fake it

A popular method of safe practice for self-harm is to use fake wounds increasingly as substitute – to satisfy the basic urges, to focus the mind on other things, to buy time in what is usually a very emotionally charged situation and to break the negative cycle. Impulsive actions and self-harm do not sit well together so the more control we exert on the situation the better. Using fake blood or fake wounds may at first seem foolish, even childish but it is a proven way to survive strong urges and to work towards reducing the practice itself. It does not work for everyone but for a high percentage it is incredibly effective. The slow considered approach and meticulous work needed to create these fake wounds help to calm a busy and distressed mind and it can easily begin to feed into established ritual. The act of creating the fake wound itself can be almost meditative in practice and the finished result can often more than satisfy the original urge. For some who practice self-harm the fake wounds have in time become their primary coping tool and offer just as much satisfaction as the 'real thing' during their transition to cessation.

The pages that follow offer recipes and instructions for some fake wounds and marks - they are not complicated – for those who wish to progress there are specialist theatrical supplies available and tuition in very complex effects online. The following pages use only items that can be found lying around in most households or bought without suspicion and use only the simplest of techniques; all of these have been real-life tested and have proven themselves effective enough to help me or people known to me deal with the intensity of self-harm urges. To do this they didn't need to be perfect, they didn't need to be movie-grade – just 'real' enough to trigger the required response. I offer them here in the hope they will help anyone ready to explore new coping tools and new ways to practice safely. Even though everything listed here is a common household item, work always with caution around things like accidental injury, allergies and skin reactions, risk of damaging clothing, utensils or furniture etc. Never apply a fake wound over the top of broken or healing skin. Take personal responsibility as you choose and use your tools and experiment with the basic techniques you learn. The resulting wounds can be very realistic once you become practiced so consider carefully the implications of presenting them to those around you as genuine injuries. This may be counterproductive. There is an element of fun to creating these fake wounds and that is OK. It is perfectly OK for a coping tool to be enjoyable. You may find yourself increasingly focused on the detail of creating better and better wounds and more and more realism but this is not in itself a bad thing – focus is good for calming the mind and settling the thoughts and swallowing up time that would otherwise have be spent on less productive, less cathartic activity. This is a coping tool that will shape itself to meet your needs and if you use it responsibly you will learn a lot about your self-harm urges and begin to better understand the thoughts and emotions attached to them. Starting to use fake wounds is a turning point in your safe practice…you may think about recording your thoughts about how your self-harm is changing as you move towards stopping..

Self-harm, secrets and lies

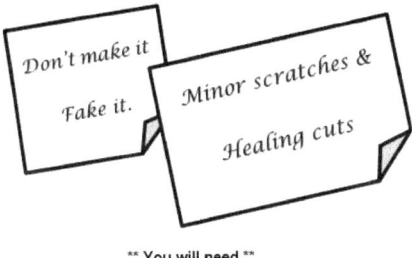

** You will need **

Medium black biro - Medium blue biro - Medium red biro
(Optional dressings and/or fake blood)

Use a free hand to hold skin taught while working if possible
Draw a red line and use the finger to smudge it out to create a faint redness along area to be used
Draw a black line in one continuous and deliberate stroke over the red and run finger from one end to other length wise with light pressure to softly smudge the line
On top of the black line use the same method to add blue
Use the red pen to add on top of this at least two solid deliberate strokes. Run the finger very lightly along the line and with tip of finger pat randomly across it.
Finally, take the black pen and draw a thin continuous line on top but not quite to the edges.
Use the tip of the finger to pat up and down or make random soft strokes.
Once the effect is achieved to not overwork it as the colours will continue to blend and illusion will be lost. This type of fake cut will fade quite quickly, especially if rubbed. It WILL transfer to clothing or bedding so be cautious.

With practice this technique can be used to create fake scratches and healing cuts but with more detailed attention to shape, size and colour, the addition of fake blood and perhaps a couple of real wound closure strips you can achieve a fresher look. When using real dressings to complement fake wounds never put them on and leave them pristine – It just isn't realistic – always use some fake blood on the underside which will show through or draw/colour in a small area and smudge it. Also slightly roughing of lifting the edges can make it look as if it has been in place for a while.

Elaine Fogarty

** You will need **

Foundation or tinted moisturiser to tone with your skin
Glue stick – Red biro – Black biro – Red felt tip pen
Pre-prepared fake blood and optional wound closure strips

In the area chosen apply a <u>very</u> light layer of foundation
Use the tip of an old biro or your fingers to apply glue to shape
(Do this in very small amounts gradually forming the raised line of the cut)
As you build, shape in the recess where 'blood' will lie

Once the ridge and recess and general shape are pleasing
Dab on a very fine layer of foundation with a soft makeup sponge and carefully blend edges.
In the recess colour a line in red felt pen or red biro
Then colour line again - this time lightly in back biro
Colour the line again in red felt pen or biro as desired.
Dot here and there with black biro
Smudge a little with the edge of a makeup sponge or finger if necessary. The effect should be quite realistic

To complete the look, use something fine to dab in fake blood
Work slowly and carefully a little here and there
Allow to settle and 'dry' into place
It can be left like this but you may wish to experiment
wound closure strips could be added and stained
Extra blood could be added if needed

This basic and quick technique uses household items
You can achieve even better results with theatrical supplies

Self-harm, secrets and lies

** You will need **

5tsp Golden syrup – 1/2tsp water – 2tsp Sifted Cornflour
4 drops Red – 1 drop Green – 1 drop Blue food colouring

In a ramekin
Add the golden syrup and the water
Mix really well to combine

Carefully add 4 drops of red food colouring
Mix well

Carefully add 1 drop green food colouring
Carefully add 1 drop blue food colouring
Mix well

(Work with extreme caution as adding too much blue)
(will ruin the colour and it will need to be started again)

Hold a fine sieve over the ramekin
Press cornflour through sieve into the ramekin and mix really well

If the consistency is not thick enough add a
little more cornflour but work with caution as
adding too much will ruin the colour and also
create an unrealistic flow consistency

This mix may mark skin or clothing – Take care.
If kept sitting for several hours this mix will start to thicken
It may be thinned by adding water 1 drop at a time

Elaine Fogarty

** You will need **

2tsp Golden syrup – 1/2tsp water – 1tsp Sifted Cornflour
6 drops Red food colouring

In a ramekin
Add the golden syrup and 6 drops of red food colouring
Mix really well to combine

Add ¼ tsp water and mix well
If needed, add another ¼ tsp water and mix well

Hold a fine sieve over the ramekin
Press cornflour through sieve into the ramekin and mix really well

This mix may mark skin or clothing – Take care

If kept sitting for several hours this mix will start to thicken
It may be thinned by adding water 1 drop at a time

Self-harm, secrets and lies

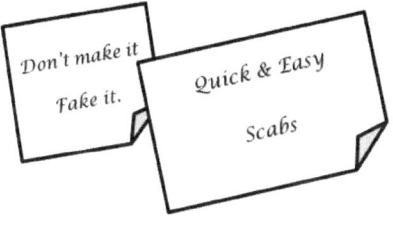

** You will need **

Cornflakes - Potted PVA glue with its own internal brush –
Lipstick in dull muted red – Bronzing powder – Yellow felt tip pen
Skin tone foundation – Golden syrup – Optional fake blood

The exact colouring of the scab can be adjusted to suit your own preference and get it as close as possible to your natural ones.

First crush the cereal to tiny irregular flakes/crumb
To dry skin apply a shape to the skin with the PVA glue
Try to make it slightly irregular.
Hold the working area over a bowl or cloth and sprinkle cereal. Tap to shake off excess and pat rest down lightly
Repeat until most parts are covered – pat lightly
It is OK to have the odd gap, perhaps even desirable.
Use a makeup sponge to transfer lipstick lightly and randomly in patches across area. Do NOT add too much. (Use eye shadow here if preferred)
Dust lightly with bronzing powder if you need a deeper colour then apply Yellow felt tip to highlight some edges and place few small random patches of yellow in the main area. Use fingertip to lightly dab on foundation over patches of the scab Leave the odd yellow area visible.

By now the PVA has started to dry…..
Use finger nail to gently lift but not break a small area away at an edge. This will add realism but to complete you need it to weep. Use something very fine to gently dab syrup under it. Do not overdo the syrup or effect will be ruined. Smudge and blend any lipstick that may remain around edges.

Elaine Fogarty

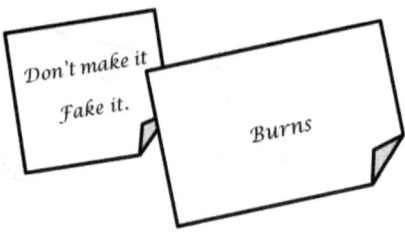

*Don't make it
Fake it.*

Burns

** You will need **

Potted PVA glue with its own internal brush – Clear lip gloss
Red eye pencil or neutral colour lipstick – Bronzing powder
Yellow felt tip pen

Paint a 10cm x 2.5cm strip of PVA on skin and allow to dry.

Use a safety pin or pinched fingernails to break open a small hole about 1/3 of the way along the line.
Tease this open to desired size and irregular shape.
Allow the 'skin' to fall and fold and wrinkle naturally.
About 1cm away make another much smaller version.
Use the red eye pencil or lipstick to apply very small amount of redness to the inside of each wound area.
Wet finger a little and smudge out to even colour.
Repeat if needed.

Darken edges of the 'raw' areas a little with red.
Apply a little yellow felt tip pen around parts of the edges and some inside the 'raw' part of the wounds – smudge to blend
Add a little yellow in dots to the wrinkled but unbroken 'skin' Press very gently with a damp finger to blend

Apply some clear lip gloss to the two 'raw' areas and a few dots of it blended into parts of surrounding 'skin'
Add a couple of very fine red dots along area between the two wounds
Blend by patting – Do not break the skin effect.
Add a dab of light yellow in fine dots around wound site if needed.
Give the whole wound site a very light dusting of bronzer
Top up the lip gloss.

Self-harm, secrets and lies

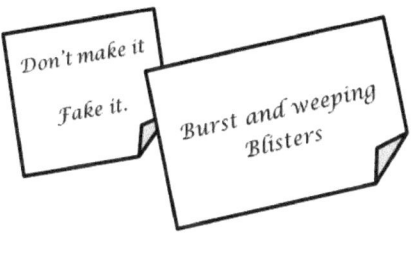

** You will need **

Light bronzing powder – Potted PVA glue with inner brush
Yellow felt tip pen – Clear lip gloss – Optional red eye pencil

---

This is a similar technique to the burn
With a large brush apply a light dusting of bronzing powder
Blow away excess and pat area with finger to bed down

Use the inner brush of the glue to paint a very thin smear
A size of approx. 5cm will usually work
Allow to dry

Locate the centre and pinch down hard to grip and break the glue
Gently tease back the edges of the glue film to form the blister area
Do not rush this

Blisters of approx. fingernail size often work best
Once happy with the shape drop edges as they fall naturally
If the film creates flaps and folds this is actually good

Use the yellow felt tip to draw a dot in the middle of the blister
Dampen fingertip and smudge the yellow out until pale
Add an optional hint of red to edge here and there then blend inward

Elaine Fogarty

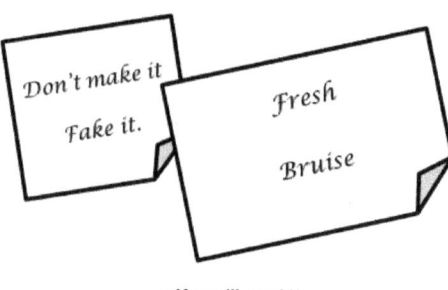

** You will need **

Red eye pencil – Royal blue or Dark Blue eye shadow

Bruises form when capillaries under the skin rupture due to impact. This is rarely even and symmetrical so you will need to recreate the random organic look if you want realism. Bruises take practice.

Apply some red eye pencil to the skin lightly forming an area about ½ your overall planned size. Blend this in circular motion with your finger or a makeup sponge to form an irregular shape.

Add more red with the pencil with a firmer touch – this time groups of dot and odd random very short line. Pat to smudge slightly and drag blend a little but do not go too far and lose the dot effect completely.

Apply only a few blue dots in the same way in 2/3 of the bruise. Pat to smudge some and towards one edge drag smudge the rest. Where the red and the blue mix it will look almost black in patches .This is ideal – do not try to correct. Finally wet your finger or a makeup sponge and in one clean motion sweep away a small patch of makeup from about ¼ of the bruise.

The void does not have to be perfect…
just soften edges.
This will add realism and illusion of swelling.
If needed add a final few red capillary dots but do not overdo.

Self-harm, secrets and lies

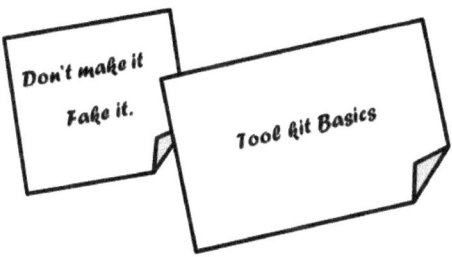

A box or a bag to safely store your items
(Use this as a starter list)
It will take practice and experimentation to develop your skills

Cotton buds and Makeup sponges
Safety pins and Make up brushes
Fine tool with spatula-like edge or old biro pen
Glue stick
Potted PVA glue with its own internal brush
Yellow felt tip pen & Fine yellow non-perm felt tip pen
Black felt tip pen & Fine black non-perm felt tip pen
Red felt tip pen & Fine red non-permanent felt tip pen
Medium blue, black red biros
Fine blue, black, red biros
Bronzing powder
Skin tone foundation
Muted pink/red lipstick and/or pen
Red and black eye pencils
Assorted eye shadow palette
(inc blue/purple/yellow/green/red)
Food colouring – red, green blue, yellow
Cornflour
Golden syrup (preferably in a squeeze bottle)
Cornflakes

Makeup removal wipes may also be useful
for clean up
Keep your kit in a cool dark dry place.

Elaine Fogarty

Harnessing ritual

Even though it often seems strange to outsiders looking in, a common thread that runs through the self-harm practice of most people is that of control – situational control and control of the self, perhaps via manipulation even an attempt at controlling others. The need to feel safe and to have control is very very strong and those of us who practice self-harm have become masters of satisfying that urge. The self-harm act itself is expression of this need but we also find control in the planning and in the preparation – ritual plays a big part in the self-harm act for a lot of people and without it there is no satisfaction achieved. This ritualistic preparation can be accepted and indeed harnessed by someone seeking to keep themselves safe and work towards minimising the need for self-harm and stopping – it can become an excellent tool in its own right... a means of transition. There is nothing wrong with ritual. It offers safety and comfort and familiarity and consistency and of course... control. Ritual can be a good thing. Harnessing this good influence means being able to build in better self-care and longer periods of distraction or coping tool substitution. Good things to add into the ritual would be a means to enable delay (even 10 or 15 minutes) so the act of self-harm itself is done with calm and clear mind rather than be driven by impulse. This could be achieved for example by the careful cleaning or sterilising and laying out of the tools. Also easy to write into the code of personal ritual would be provision of a first aid box and a phone with emergency numbers programmed in. Even if they were never needed, their presence would become accepted and eventually necessary. The contents of a kit ritualistically laid out could also include materials to fake wounds or small easy to use coping tools to distract or to provide either sensation or visual options beyond physical harm. Again, these may not be used but regular and prominent presence would develop options for self-care.

Self-harm, secrets and lies

A notebook and pen is a good addition to any toolbox as it offers a chance to express the intense feelings safely. Ritual enables the practice and the practice informs the ritual – by harnessing the power of our personal rituals we can begin to reshape our self-harm practice while at the same time shifting focus more and more towards self-care and cessation.

Ritual isn't always about the physical world - our self-talk and our thought processes can also be laced with strong ritualistic elements – in the emotionally charged moments prior to self-harm this ritualistic self-talk is at its most persuasive. The good news is that this can be harnessed too and deliberate positive influences on such thinking is not only possible but relatively easy to learn. Some approach this formally via therapy such as Cognitive behavioural therapy and some by more intuitive conversations with their inner selves – it does not matter how the little pockets of change are interwoven with existing ritual – it is simply enough that they are. Everyone can find ways to harness their own ritual behaviours and to weave self-care and personal responsibility and personal growth into them.

It is entirely possible.

Elaine Fogarty

Self-harm, secrets and lies

Lifeline (N. Ireland)
0808 808 8000   www.lifelinehelpline.info
(24/7/365 - Crisis Support line)

(Lifeline's professional counsellors are experienced in working with trauma, suicide, self-harm, abuse, depression and anxiety. Other local community counselling may be arranged by them if needed) You may also ring Lifeline with concerns about the wellbeing of someone else who you believe to be struggling with these issues

Childline
0800 1111   www.childline.org.uk
(24/7/365 – No problem to big or small)

(Childline is a totally confidential service for children and young people up to 19.
Calls do not appear on phone bills from home or most mobiles.)

Samaritans
FREE - 116 123   www.samaritans.org
(24/7/365 – Crisis Support line)

Calls are taken by fully trained members of the public who are committed to offering a totally confidential 'listening ear' service to anyone in distress. Under 18s may also call without fear of unwanted family/guardian involvement.

The International Association for Suicide Prevention
www.iasp.info/resources/Crisis_Centres/

Simply clicking on the provided map on this website will link you to a list of crisis support resource centres in your country.

GP's and school counsellors will be able to offer information and direct you to other support sources locally. You may also wish to speak with a trusted friend, professional, community leader or spiritual leader.

**Remember you are never alone –
Help and information are available both in times of crisis and when working to manage your self-harm or any mental health condition.**

Elaine Fogarty

You may wish to check out the following websites

(Listed alphabetically as examples for information only)
(Many other excellent sites available. Not all are UK based)

www.changeyourmindni.org

www.hscni.net

www.mentalhealth.org.uk

www.mentalhealthrecovery.com

www.mind.org.uk

www.mindingyourhead.info

www.nhs.uk

www.rcpsych.ac.uk

www.rethink.org

www.sane.org

www.selfharm.co.uk

www.thementalhealthforum.co.uk

www.youngminds.org.uk

Elaine Fogarty

A map of my own support structure

Self-harm, secrets and lies

My ideas for future Self-Care

Elaine Fogarty

Self-harm, secrets and lies

Elaine Fogarty

My emergency Tool box…

✎ Choose a box or a bag or a drawer – whatever feels right Put into it the things that will help you cope when you next have the urge to self-harm. These can be items to help as coping tools or written notes, photos, anything that is personally relevant. Write a list here of things you would include and then set aside some time to actually create your emergency tool box.

My Safe Practice Checklist…

Have to hand…
Tools to help cope with urge to self-harm
Appropriately stocked personal first aid kit
Appropriately stocked and hygienic self-harm tool kit, Information on how to self-treat various self-injury types (See section on safe practice) Money to pay for taxi if needed for non-emergency help (Do not drive – you may be affected in unexpected ways)
Phone numbers for emotional/practical support

Seek emergency help immediately if…
You have taken an overdose
You have ingested a poison
Your breathing is compromised
You have severe chest pain
Blood is spurting from the wound
Your tool breaks and part becomes lodged inside a wound
You have cut deep enough to expose muscle
You have a burn on somewhere sensitive like face, palm or a joint
You have a chemical burn of any kind
You have in any way damaged the eyes
You have bleeding which won't stop
You have loss of sensation around the area of harm
You have loss of sensation anywhere else
You have cold clammy skin, persistent dizziness or rapid pulse
Your wound or burn is larger than 6cm in size
You notice days later any swelling, weeping, foul smell or aching

My own emergency contact numbers

....

....

....

....

....

....

....

....

Personal Notes

Elaine Fogarty

Self-harm, secrets and lies

Elaine Fogarty

Self-harm, secrets and lies

Elaine Fogarty

Self-harm, secrets and lies

Elaine Fogarty

Self-harm, secrets and lies

bipolarlainey@hotmail.co.uk
Follow @bipolarlainey
www.facebook.com/bipolarlainey
Search Facebook for @eveningcbt

**Check out my blog
bipolarlainey.wordpress.com**
and my other book
"Diary of a bipolar survivor"
(Available on Amazon)

www.diaryofabipolarsurvivor.com

**No personal income is taken from sale of this book.
All Royalties earned will be donated to**

(The Southern Health & Social Care Trust Area – NI)
Charity number: NIC104166

The Mental Health Forum continues to be a most valued source of support, empowerment, encouragement and inspiration to me. I couldn't have developed my role as advocate for mental health discussion without this group and it plays a big part in my recovery journey and personal growth.
Our group is recognised as the official independent Service user voice in Statutory mental health services within The Southern Health & Social Care Trust (NI) contributing to multiple levels of decision-making, planning and provision of care.

**Our website launched October 2015
www.thementalhealthforum.co.uk**

Elaine Fogarty

Special thanks also extended to Emma

for her support during times of challenge and friendship without veneer.

And

to Carole for patience and kind assistance during development of this book, peers who gave up time to review early drafts, and family who offered the encouragement and support needed to make this book a reality

www.ingramcontent.com/pod-product-compliance
Lightning Source LLC
Chambersburg PA
CBHW060516100426
42743CB00009B/1338